For Purpose and Pleasure

— *For* —
Purpose and Pleasure

Quilting Together in
Nineteenth-Century America

———

Sandi Fox

RUTLEDGE HILL PRESS

NASHVILLE, TENNESSEE

Published in Nashville, Tennessee, by Rutledge Hill Press, Inc., 211 Seventh Avenue North, Nashville, Tennessee 37219

Typography by D&T/Bailey Typesetting, Inc., Nashville, Tennessee
Design by Harriette Bateman

Photography Credits: Photographs of the quilts and bedcovers in the collection of the Los Angeles County Museum of Art are primarily by Steve Oliver, to whom I am additionally grateful for his advice, counsel, and friendship. The photographs of the Asylum quilt and Sister Hattie Nye's quilt are by Ron Reed. Photographs of the Bear Lake Stake quilt, and of all other quilts loaned to the exhibition, are by Jim Frankowski at Borge Anderson and Associates. Unless otherwise indicated, all other photographs are reproduced courtesy of the owner.

Excerpts from *Far From Home: Families of the Westward Journey* reprinted by permission of the publisher, Pantheon Books. © 1989 by the authors, Lillian Schlissel, Byrd Gibbens, and Elizabeth Hampsten.

Library of Congress Cataloging-in-Publication Data

Fox, Sandi.
    For purpose and pleasure : quilting together in nineteenth-century America / Sandi Fox.
        p. cm.
    "Published in conjunction with the exhibition . . . presented at the Utah Museum of Fine Arts, University of Utah, June 25 through September 10, 1995"—T.p. verso.
    Includes bibliographical references and index.
    ISBN 1–55853–337–0
    1. Material culture—United States—History—19th century—Exhibitions. 2. Quilts—United States—History—19th century—Exhibitions.   3. Women—United States—History—19th century—Exhibitions.   4. Social group work—United States—History—19th century—Exhibitions.   5. United States—Social life and customs—19th century.   I. Utah Museum of Fine Arts.   II. Title.
GN432.F69 1995   95–12014
746.46'0973'09034—dc20   CIP

Printed in Hong Kong through Palace Press
1 2 3 4 5 6 7 8 — 99 98 97 96 95

Contents

Acknowledgments vii
Note to the Reader ix
Preface xi

1 Quilting Frame   *3*
How Much I Prize My Album Patch-Work   *15*
Please to Accept This Token of My Affection   *21*
Scribed and Stenciled, Stamped and Stitched   *27*
Presented by the Ladies   *35*
Baltimore's Own   *51*
I Lay My Body Down to Sleep   *63*
Mother   *71*
Gently Rest Beneath These Pieces Joined by Friendly Hands for Thee   *83*
Woman's Work Is Never Done   *97*
For God Loveth a Cheerful Giver   *107*
And Departed This Life   *115*
Dear Little Charlie   *119*
When Next You Come Who Will You Be   *127*
When Thou Art Gone to Western Land   *133*
I Think I Will Sirtenly Get Insane   *143*
My Quilted Self   *147*
To Labor in God's Vineyard   *157*

Bibliography 160
Index 163

For purpose,

for pleasure,

for John.

The Emmaus Church Quilt (detail)
Made for Dr. John G. Carter by
the ladies of the Emmaus Church
New Kent County, Virginia
1852
101 x 86 in. (256.6 x 218.4 cm)
Valentine Museum

Acknowledgments

I have long been fascinated by the social history surrounding women quilting together in nineteenth-century America, and I am very grateful to Frank Sanguinetti, director of the Utah Museum of Fine Arts, for the opportunity to organize an exhibition of the extraordinary quilts and bedcovers that were the result of their collaborative efforts. It was a great pleasure to work with Charles Loving during the initial stages of the project, and thereafter with Allison South, assistant director, and David Carroll, registrar. I am particularly indebted to those individuals and institutions who so generously loaned objects from their distinguished collections: Darwin Bearley, Byron and Sara Dillow, Laura Fisher, Los Angeles County Museum of Art, Lynn Historical Society, Museum of Church History and Art, Paul Pilgrim and Gerald Roy, and Stella Rubin.

The illustration of additional objects and comparative material owes much to a distinguished group of colleagues, curators and collectors, registrars and research librarians, dealers and friends. The publication is enhanced by the images and by their participation:

Barbara Luck of the Abby Aldrich Rockefeller Folk Art Center; Joel and Kate Kopp of America Hurrah Antiques NYC; Linda Baumgarten, Ronald L. Hurst, Kimberly Smith Ivey, and Catherine Grosfils of the Colonial Williamsburg Foundation; Colwill-McGehee; Tom Cuff; Nancy Tuckhorn of the DAR Museum; Pat Ferrero; James and Nancy Glazer; David Hewett; Hirschl & Adler; Edith Menna of International Society Daughters of Utah Pioneers, Pioneer Memorial Museum; Library of Congress; Los Angeles County Museum of Art; Laurel Nilsen and Ken Turino of the Lynn Historical Society; Lois Swanee of the Marshall County Historical Museum; Glenna Merrill; Johanna Metzgar of the Museum of Early Southern Decorative Arts; Mr. and Mrs. Thomas H. Morgan; Gloria Scoville of the Museum of Church History and Art; Oregon Historical Society; private collectors in Los Angeles and New York City; Dilys Blum of the Philadelphia Museum of Art; Marguerite Riordan; Society for the Preservation of New England Antiquities; Nancy Druckman of Sotheby's, New York City; Richard Stringfellow of the Tippecanoe County Historical Association;

Gail Andrews Trechsel of the Birmingham Museum of Art; United Yarn Products; Utah State Historical Society; Colleen Callahan of the Valentine Museum; Marguerite Wiebusch; Karol A. Schmiegel of Winterthur; and Ann Ziol.

The same careful attention given to my first book with Rutledge Hill Press by my publisher, Lawrence Stone, by my editor, Amy Lyles Wilson, and by its designer, Harriette Bateman, has been lavished also on this second. I am grateful to them all, and to my agent, Rita Rosenkranz.

Among the inscriptions on an 1855 New Jersey quilt (no. 177) made for Cornelia Baird Hoagland, her sister, Catherine, has written:

> It is not when our path is bright,
> That friends are put to test;
> But in the gloom of sorrow's night
> We know who loves us best.

One hundred and forty years later, I know that to still be true. Helen Bing, Maggie Murray, and Carolyn Wagner will understand why I wish to acknowledge their very special contribution to *For Purpose and Pleasure: Quilting Together in Nineteenth-Century America.*

Note to the Reader

The surfaces of these quilts and bedcovers are rich with written words, with inscriptions and verses, with signatures and dates, and with towns and villages occasionally no longer found on maps. Although every effort has been made for complete and accurate transcriptions, much has been rendered illegible through chemistry and circumstances.

Diaries and journals have been quoted extensively and grammar, punctuation, and spelling are presented as they occur. Old-style lettering, such as "Mifs" for "Miss," has been retained.

Except where it is called out in the text or caption or is obvious to the reader's eye, the quilts and bedcovers are primarily tabby- or plain-weave cotton. Measurements appear both in inches and in centimeters, and length precedes width.

*T*his book was published in conjunction with the exhibition *For Purpose and Pleasure: Quilting Together in Nineteenth-Century America* presented at the Utah Museum of Fine Arts, University of Utah, June 25 through September 10, 1995.

Lenders to the exhibition:

Darwin D. Bearley Antiques, Akron, Ohio
Dr. Byron and Sara Dillow, Fremont, Nebraska
Laura Fisher/Antique Quilts and Americana, New York City
Los Angeles County Museum of Art, Los Angeles, California
Lynn Historical Society, Lynn, Massachusetts
Museum of Church History and Art, Salt Lake City, Utah
Pilgrim/Roy, Oakland, California
Stella Rubin Antiques, Potomac, Maryland

The exhibition was supported by the National Endowment for the Arts and by a grant from Mrs. Helen Bing.

Preface

American women have always quilted together, for purpose and for pleasure, and it is the purpose of this book and the pleasure of this author to present and discuss an important selection of those nineteenth-century American quilts and bedcovers that were the results of their cooperative and creative labors. Either subtly or specifically, these were the American quilts that confirmed the importance of family and friendship, commemorated rites of passage, were presented to preachers and presidents, traveled west with the pioneers, and used as fundraisers for churches and for the great social causes of the nineteenth century.

In addition to their aesthetic merit, American quilts are increasingly valued as significant articles of our material culture, and particularly when their surfaces bear names and dates and inscriptions, they can be evaluated as important social documents as well. Those quilts that were, to a large or lesser degree, the work of many hands are interpreted in paintings and in prints, in papers and periodicals contemporary to the period, in vintage photographs, and in the oral traditions from which American myths are made. Significantly, there is also a hand-written record, set down in eighteenth- and nineteenth-century diaries, journals, and remembrances. From these rich resources, and from the objects themselves, we can begin to more fully understand the women who participated in that domestic ritual and the unique nature of the extraordinary quilts they worked together.

Quilting
Harper's Weekly, 13 April 1861

For Purpose and Pleasure

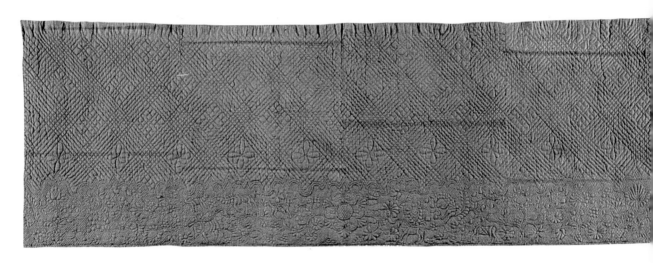

1. Petticoat
   Colonial America
   Mid-eighteenth century
   Los Angeles County Museum of Art
   Costume Council Fund

1 Quilting Frame

The historical precedent for quilting together in America in the nineteenth century was recorded in the diaries and journals of the eighteenth century. Relatively few existing quilts from that earlier period are firmly documented as having been worked with friends; one notable exception is a whole-cloth, pale blue silk quilt, made within the Quaker community, bearing a quilted inscription along its top edge: "Drawn by Sarah Smith Sti[t]ched by Hannah Callendar and Catherine Smith in Testimony of their Friendship 10 mo 5th 1761."[1]

There are more than eighty references to quilting in the Massachusetts diary that Elizabeth Porter Phelps began in 1763[2] and continued for the rest of her life. Although those references are characterized by their brevity, they are nevertheless sufficient to support the terminology suggested in a number of similar documents. We can determine, for example, that Elizabeth's frequently used phrase "a quilting" was applied to clothing as well as to bedquilts. In that period, a "quilt" often referred to a quilted petticoat (nos. 1 and 2), and that would seem to be the case in her 19 April 1767 entry, ". . . came here Miss Pen and Miss Polly to help me quilt a dark brown quilt,"[3] and that of 8 June 1767 when ". . .Sally Goodrich came here to help me quilt;. . . at night Miss Patty came to help me. Thursday about noon we finished the quilt (twas a black one for mother)."[4]

Although it is not always the case in these early diaries, Elizabeth does differentiate between the various objects of their efforts, and bedquilts seem to be quite consistently described as such: "went to quilt upon a bed-quilt for my aunt Porter" (August 1769); "Mama to Aunt Marshes to Quilt on Phebes Bed Quilt" (September 1773); "sister here. . . .we Quilted Penes Bed quilt" (December 1781); "Pene and I at Coll'l Porters to quilt on a bed Quilt for Jerusha Phillips" (October 1783); "sister and I went to Mr. Hop, to quilt on Pollys bed Quilt. Fryday I at the Coll'l to help Mrs. Porter quilt hers" (September 1785); "up at Mr. Worthingtons to Quilt a bed Quilt — we got it done and got home Just after nine" (November 1786); "sister Warner here to help me quilt on a Bed quilt" (April 1787); "sister Warner here in the morn to help me Quilt a Bedquilt for Sister Dickinson" (September 1788); and "sister Warner and Mrs. Shipman here to help me Quilt a Bed quilt for Porter. Fryday here again. Satt. Porter got home — the Bed-quilt got off just at night" (October 1788).

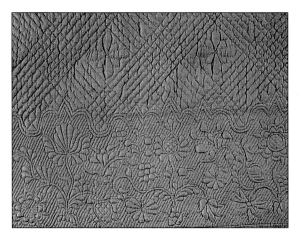

2. Petticoat (detail)

Although Elizabeth Phelps identifies the participants and the objects, there are few physical descriptions of those "bed quilts": in 1797, "Mrs. Hitchcock & I put on her red & blue bed quilt,"[5] and in 1800, "Put on the frame a small bed quilt. Fryday Quilted it,"[6] and "Susan Cutler here in the morning to tarry . . . & help us Quilt Betsy['s] Copper plate bed quilt."[7]

In Hadley, Massachusetts, it was the quilting frame that provided a common arena of activity,[8] and there were similar scenes up and down the eastern seaboard. An extensive circle of family and friends quilted with Frances Baylor Hill at Hillsborough, her home in King and Queen County, Virginia, where across the quilting frame they could look through the rows of crepe myrtle across a wide expanse of lawn, on down to the Mattaponi River. Almost all we know of those domestic days at Hillsborough, and indeed of Frances herself, is contained in her journal, begun on the first day of January 1797: "Having a bad memory I write this Journal that I may with pleasure at the end of the year know who & what I have seen, where I have been & what I have been employ'd about, &c&c"[9] and noting at the

end of that year, on Sunday, December 31, "And now make a conclusion of my journal which has been rather more tedious that I suppos'd it would have been when I first began."[10] If Elizabeth Phelps's diary is remarkable for its length, Frances's is distinguished by the detail and delight contained in its considerably fewer pages.

During the last week of July, Frances records on Monday, that while "Cousin A G continu'd to be very sick I made two caps for Cousin E Taylors child, Aunt Temple very busy fiscing her bedquilt in the frame," and on Tuesday, "help'd to make gingerbread and Bisquit — wash'd & iron'd 3 pieces of muslin and quilt'd a little in the evening."[11] By the following day, quilting together began in earnest.

Wednesday. Aunt Temple and my-self went to work on the quilt by times, we had Cousin P Gwathmey [,] Camm Garlick, Nancy & Becky Aylett, Mrs & Miss

3. The Flowering Tree Quilt (detail)
Possibly Hillsborough Plantation, King and Queen County, Virginia
First quarter nineteenth century
92 x 81 in. (233.7 x 205.7 cm)
Valentine Museum, gift of Mrs. Edward J. Mosley Jr.

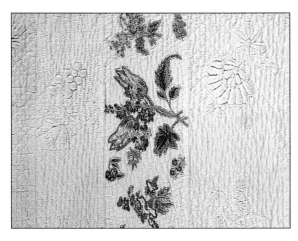

4. *Quilting Frolic*
John Lewis Krimmel
1813
Oil
16⅞ x 22⅜ in. (42.9 x 56.8 cm)
Courtesy, Winterthur Museum

Polly Turner, Miss Caty Pollard & Mrs Simons to help us, we quilt'd a great deal and was very merry The Ladies all went away at night but Camm & Cuz Polly, we had Sam Garlick to plague us, at night John Hill came, we also had the Miss Temples to help us and staid all night.

Thursday. Miss Caty Pollard came back to help us again, we did not do so much to day as we did yesterday, Cousin Nancy very sick not able to quilt a stitch, we had a number of fine water mellons & Peach's a plenty of Bisquit & Cake fine eating and merry quilting.

Friday. Mrs. Garlick & Sally came had no other company, we spent the day agreable eating drinking and quilting, Cousin John Hill, Sam Garlick, & Cousin Ben Temple draw'd on the quilt . . .

Saturday. Aunt Gwathmey came to Breakfast, we got the quilt out early in the day and then the girls all went to making edging.[12]

If the particulars of those July entries add to our knowledge of the social aspects of quilting together in America in the closing years of the eighteenth century, they also add to our knowledge of the quiltmaking terminology of that period. Frances speaks very specifically of "bed quilts" during this and other occasions, but additional entries speak of her own project as a "counterpain." In May, while on a visit to "Row Mount," she

5. *The Quilting Party*
   Artist unidentified
   Probably 1854–75
   Oil and pencil on paper adhered to plywood
   19¼ x 26⅛ in. (48.9 x 66.4 cm)
   Abby Aldrich Rockefeller Folk Art Center,
   Williamsburg, Virginia

works on it alone: "had no company read & work'd a little on the counterpain," and "work'd on my counterpain wrote a song & read a little in gays fables walk'd out in the evening."[13] "Uneasy" because of the news of an outbreak of smallpox at Hillsborough, she busied herself by working "a great many leaves on my counterpain."[14] Returning home, and following the dangers and deaths from the epidemic, her friends began to join her efforts, and in the telling of their assistance Frances gives a clue as to the counterpain itself: "the young Ladys still continu'd to work for me they fill'd up a great many leaves very pretty."[15]

Although probably worked somewhat later than Frances's "counterpain," the flowers and leaves (no. 3) on the surface of a quilt with a Hillsborough attribution[16] suggest a tradition there of the technique of *broderie perse* (motifs cut from chintz and appliquéd onto a solid ground) and stuffed-work quilting. That she refers to her piece as a "counterpain" rather than a "quilt" would seem to suggest it is an all-white work, probably Marseilles quilting done without an overall batting, in which the outline of that leafy design is quilted through two layers of cloth, the bottom fabric of a very slightly looser weave than that of the top; the principle motifs are then "fill'd up," or stuffed through slightly parted threads from the reverse. Her solitary work on the piece continues ("Thursd Fryday work'd on my Counterpain saw no company only an old Gentleman or two."[17]) as does communal effort ("Sister

6. *A Quilting Party in Western Virginia* from *Gleason's Pictorial Drawing-Room Companion,* 21 October 1854
Reproduced from the Collections of the Library of Congress

Nancy help'd me work 4 or 5 days on my Counterpain"[18]) until at last, on 31 December 1797: "I finish'd my Counterpain on Saturday which has been about 3 year."[19] The journal is completed also, and it alone remains.

In her description of those "merry quiltings" at Hillsborough, Frances Baylor Hill's journal is consistent with entries in other diaries of the period, and indeed with our twentieth-century perception of those occasions. In Maine, in 1790, Martha Ballard recorded that "My girls had some neighbours to help them quilt a bed quilt, 15 ladies. They began to quilt at 3 hour pm. Finisht and took it out at 7 evening. There were 12 gentlemen took tea. They danced a little while after supper. Behaved exceedingly clever . . ."[20] Such "exceedingly clever" behavior was the subject of John Lewis Krimmel's 1813 painting *Quilting Frolic* (no. 4). A floor littered with scraps of fabric indicates

that woman's work has been done. Amid a substantial accumulation of material objects (pewter, ceramic cups, knives, and forks, for example), servants attempt to restore order as the gentlemen arrive for the concluding phase of the day's activities; while refreshments are being prepared, the quilt that was the impetus for the gathering has been completed and is being taken off the frame. Certainly the costumes would have changed, and the interior, but the scene is not unlike the occasion described by Sarah Davenport almost four decades later, in 1852, in New Canaan, Connecticut: "Cousin and I have been up to Uncle's to the quilting party. There was a quite a large number there and this evening quite a party of ladies and Gentleman were there."[21] And perhaps, as he had done earlier, "Sandy [had come] also with his Fiddle and we all danced till we were tiard then eat some refreshment."[22]

Another painting (no. 5), by an unidentified artist, has widely shaped our visual concept of the physical circumstances of "quiltings." This interior is certainly less grand, albeit including painted window

7. *Husking Bee,* from *Harper's Weekly,* 13 November 1858

shades, and the sparse contents include primarily a variety of rather common chairs and stools. Several of the *Quilting Party* participants, particularly the fervent suitor at the far right, are closer to the image of the country bumpkin that had been subtly introduced to the image of rural Americans. As with a significant number of paintings, drawings, and schoolgirl embroideries,[23] this icon of American folk art was in fact copied from a print source, in this instance an engraved composition, *A Quilting Party in Western Virginia* (no. 6) from *Gleason's Pictorial Drawing-Room Companion* (21 October 1854).

Such group activities as quilting parties, husking bees (no. 7), and apple parings (no. 8) provided authors with subject matter and illustrators with a rich source of popular imagery for such periodicals and publications as *Godey's Lady's Book* (no. 9) and *Harper's Weekly* (no. 10). (As indicated by diaries and journals of the period, the quiltings held contemporaneous to those other activities were referred to as "quiltings," quilting "parties," or quilting "frolics"; refer-

9. *Quilting Party,* from *Godey's Lady's Book,* September 1849

8. *Apple Bee,* drawn by Winslow Homer, from *Harper's Weekly,* 26 November 1859

ences to quilting "bees" seem not to occur until the second half of the century.) And these collaborative festivities were particular favorites of such genre painters as John Krimmel and William Sidney Mount.

There is a quieter image of quilting together in America in the nineteenth century, this by genre specialist Enoch Wood Perry. His were most often the nostalgic scenes of domestic virtues. A wood engraving of his solitary quiltmaker appeared in *Harper's Weekly* in 1872 (no. 11); four years later that same figure sat in her Windsor chair, joined by another woman at her quilting frame (no. 12). Her younger companion has paused, perhaps to listen, but in her hands she holds the essentials of the craft, with a spool of thread in her right hand and, dimly seen beneath the quilting frame, a needle in her left. Genre paintings are defined by their presentation of the commonplace, some

10. *The "Brothers" Assisted in the Quilting*, from
Harper's Weekly, 21 April 1883

"homely moment of life"[24] painted by an artist contemporary to the period he has reproduced. Earlier accepted as accurate documentation of America's yesterdays, current scholarship now more generally recognizes such scenes as Krimmel's *Quilting Frolic* as composite moments intended to reflect those cultural values by which America wished to be defined. But if Perry had wished to perpetuate America's domestic myths, in this instance he has nevertheless captured its realities.

In colonial America, the quilt was often already on the frame when family and friends arrived to stitch together its multiple layers. In this particular exchange of labor, a concept integral to preindustrial America, creativity was often secondary to companionship. By the middle of the nineteenth century, however, women had more fully involved themselves with the surfaces of those quilts they would complete together, particularly in the construction of album and friendship quilts, but even at that century's end, the simple circumstances of "quilting together" seem to have remained constant. Of his boyhood in Kansas, J. J. Propps (born 1886) remembered:

There was very little social life on the farm for the adults and older people. Sometimes the women would have quilting parties. When some woman had her quilt sewn together and had the lining fastened to the quilting frames ready for the batting and top to be put on, she would let it be known that she would welcome help . . . . The women would gather around the four sides of the frames — often suspended from the ceiling — the batting would be spread on the lining, and then the top fastened loosely over it. Each woman would make short even stitches through lining, batting and top usually in a curving design, marked on with chalk, as far as she could reach. Then they would take the long metal pins from the corners of the frames and roll the two longer sides toward the middle bringing the unquilted parts within reach of the sewing fingers. The pins would be replaced and the women would proceed with their curving stitches. This was repeated as often as necessary to finish the quilting. A good fast group could finish a quilt in one day, including removing [it] from the frames and binding the edges by hand. Needless to say, much visiting and gossiping accompanied the quilting party and a good lunch was always served.[25]

Men often recorded the memories of quiltings held in their mothers' homes. William Allen White remembered the women of Butler County, Kansas, in the late 1860s and early 1870s who had

left homes of culture in many cases, left sheltered circles and many of the softening influences of civilization which are dear to women — dearer than to men, perhaps — and had come out to the

desolate, wind-swept prairie town where they were too frequently poorly-housed, roughly fed, and more lonesome than anyone will ever know, unless some day he reads between the lines of the hopeful letters that these brave women sent back East — letters wherein they tried so hard to put the best foot forward, to conceal the disagreeable truth. . . . Life was full of drudgery too often, and disheartening. They came here little more than brides — did the women who used to gather around my mother's quilting frame in those first few years. The faces that were lit up by the candles that sat on the corners of the frame, or upon the quilt, were young faces in those days. . . only a few of them were scarred by

11. Wood Engraving
E. Wood Perry
Harper's Weekly, 21 December 1872

12. *Quilting Party*
E. Wood Perry
1876
Oil
25 x 30¼ in. (63.5 x 76.8 cm)
Courtesy of Marguerite Riordan, Stonington,
Connecticut

wrinkles then. The picture comes up so vividly to me as photographed upon a child's brain.[26]

At the end of the century, another group has paused as a photographer records them and the object of their labor (no. 13). There in the arbor, now only dimly seen, they are quilting together—for purpose and for pleasure.

NOTES

1. Collection of Independence National Historical Park. Illustrated in Jane Bentley Kolter, *Forget Me Not: A Gallery of Friendship and Album Quilts* (New York: Sterling, 1990), 11.
2. For several months the entries in Elizabeth's diary recorded only the names of the ministers preaching in the meeting house she attended, along with a brief note on the text and the biblical chapter and verse. But three years later, at a specific moment in her young life, the style and content of her diary were altered:

    October 26. This day when I got to the meeting house heard of the Death of the Wife of Samuel Gaylord .... This Mr. Samuel Gaylord Junior of Hadley Was Married to Submit Dickingson of Hatfield on the 17 of April 1766. On October 19 She was Delivered of a child but Dead born;

13. Photograph, Mehama Quilting Bee
     Circa 1900
     Oregon State Historical Society, neg. no. OrHi
     21876

She continued to appearance comfortable till the next Thursday from that time grew very bad. Died on Satterday night.

Even though Samuel and Submit had eventually married, to have conceived that child still out of wedlock would have born serious social and civil consequences, such as those documented by Melinde Lutz Sanborn in *Lost Babes: Fornication Abstracts from Court Records, Essex County, Massachusetts 1692–1745* (Derry, NH: n.p., 1992), and the following Sunday Elizabeth listened to the reading of "a very humble confession [by Samuel Gaylord] for being guilty of the sin of fornication . . . so that this malloncholly instance might be a warning to all."

With those events, in the month that she turned nineteen, she became increasingly aware of her own mortality ("In the afternoon we went to see Miss Electy Ellis who is now in her twentieth year and appears to be just gone in a consumption. Death regards not any age. . . . About seven oclock this morning Died Electy Ellis of Hatfield. The Voice to all is be ye also ready?") and her diary entries became a more fully recorded history of her life and of Hadley, Massachusetts. It was in that more secular context she now entered in her diary her first reference to quilting: "This day have been a quilting for my Aunt Marsh." Elizabeth Porter Phelps. "The Diary of Elizabeth (Porter) Phelps." Edited by Thomas Eliot Andrews. *The New England Historical and Genealogical Register* 118 (1964): 13–14.

3. Ibid., 15. For additional information and illustrations of these early quilted petticoats, see Linda Baumgarten, *Eighteenth-Century Clothing at Williamsburg* (Williamsburg, VA: Colonial Williamsburg Foundation, 1986), and Sandi Fox, *Wrapped in Glory: Figurative Quilts & Bedcovers 1700–1900* (New York: Thames and Hudson/Los Angeles County Museum of Art, 1990), 36–37.

4. Ibid., 16. Black "quilts" would seem to have been appropriate for all ages. At age 10, young

Anna Green Winslow (having been sent to Boston to be "finished" in Boston schools) wrote to her Mamma, "I want to know whether I may give my old black quilt to Mrs Kuhn, for aunt sais, it is never worth while to take the pains to mend it again." Anna Green Winslow, *Diary of Anna Green Winslow: A Boston School Girl of 1771.* Edited by Alice Morse Earle. (Boston: Houghton, Mifflin, 1894), 5.

5. Phelps, "Diary," January 1967, 61.

6. Phelps, "Diary," October 1967, 299.

7. Ibid., 303. For illustrations and a fine, concise text on early English and French copperplate-printed textiles, see Gillian Moss, *Printed Textiles 1760–1860 in the Collection of the Cooper-Hewitt Museum* (Washington, DC: Smithsonian Institution, 1987), 16–24. These pictorial toiles, usually monochromatic, were primarily used as furnishing fabrics, and the number of extant whole-cloth quilts incorporating these elegant textiles suggests their great popularity.

8. It is not unusual that this valuable piece of domestic equipment should appear in early inventories and wills: in Virginia, for example, from an inventory of the estate of Mrs. Eliza Stanard, deceased, "1 Quilting frame." (Middlesex County, Virginia, *Will Book C, 1740–1748,* p. 379, 30 July 1747) and from an appraisement of the estate of Benjamin Marrable, deceased, "1 Quilting Frame." (Charles City County, Virginia, *Record, 1766–1774,* p. 459, 22 April 1773.) Research facilities, Museum of Early Southern Decorative Arts.

9. Frances Baylor Hill, "The Diary of Frances Baylor Hill (1797), of 'Hillsborough,' King and Queen County, Virginia." Edited by William K. Bottorff and Roy C. Flannagan. *Early American Literature Newsletter* 2, no. 3 (Winter 1967), 6.

10. Hill, *Diary,* 53.

11. Ibid., 38.

12. Ibid.

13. Ibid., 30.

14. Ibid., 31.

15. Ibid., 41.

16. For further illustration and a detailed discussion of this quilt, see Sandi Fox, *Wrapped in Glory,* 24–27.

17. Hill, *Diary,* 51.

18. Ibid., 52.

19. Ibid., 53.

20. Quoted in Laurel Thatcher Ulrich, *A Midwife's Tale: The Life of Martha Ballard, Based on Her Diary 1785–1812* (New York: Vintage, 1991), 146.

21. Sarah Davenport, "The Journal of Sarah Davenport: May 1, 1849 Through May 26, 1852." *New Canaan Historical Society* 2 (1950): 86.

22. Ibid., 43. The black fiddler appears in a number of other genre paintings: William Sidney Mount's *Rustic Dance After a Sleigh Ride,* for example (1830, collection of Museum of Fine Arts, Boston). For additional information on this figure, see Sarah Burns, *Pastoral Inventions: Rural Life in Nineteenth-Century American Art and Culture* (Philadelphia: Temple University, 1989), 130–35.

23. A number of examples are illustrated and discussed in *American Folk Paintings: Paintings and Drawings Other Than Portraits from the Abby Aldrich Rockefeller Folk Art Center.* The Abby Aldrich Rockefeller Folk Art Center Series, edited by Beatrice T. Rumford, no. 2. (Boston: Little, Brown, 1988), Chapter V, "Literary and Historical Subjects."

24. Hermann Warner Williams Jr., *Mirror to the American Past: A Survey of American Genre Painting: 1750–1900* (Greenwich, CT: New York Graphics Society, 1973), 17.

25. J. J. Propps, "My Childhood and Youth in Arkansas," *Arkansas Historical Quarterly* 26, no.4 (Winter 1967): 351–52.

26. White, William Allen. "The 'Quilting Bee' Crowd," in *History of Butler County, Kansas.* Edited by Vol. P. Mooney. (Lawrence, KS: Standard Publishing, 1916), 329–30.

14. *Lovers in a Garden,* from *Orbis Pictus*
Lewis Miller
Pennsylvania, circa 1849
Watercolor and ink on paper
9¹¹⁄₁₆ x 7⅞ in. (24.6 x 20 cm)
Colonial Williamsburg Foundation, Williams-
burg, Virginia

How Much I Prize My Album Patch-Work

*T*housands remain of the watercolor and ink drawings through which Lewis Miller (1796–1882) recorded America.[1] His work chronicled the ordinary with extraordinary accuracy and celebrated the commonplace with uncommon charm, and both characteristics are evident in his drawing of lovers in a garden (no. 14). That scene and its accompanying verse are a page from his *Orbis Pictus*, the title page (no. 15) of which identifies the handbound book as "A picturesque / Album / To the Ladies / of York.. Pennsylvania.. / the 1th. day of January. 1849." In the suggestion of a leafy bower, the lovers sit upon painted "fancy" chairs, typically stenciled, with elements of freehand embellishment. Seemingly ignoring both her gentleman caller and the valentine[2] he has given her, the young woman knits endlessly, with the accouterments of her handwork near by: sewing basket, scissors, ball of yarn, and a pedestal pincushion that echoes the shape of the table on which they have all been placed. The exactness of Miller's rendering has allowed Ronald L. Hurst, curator of furniture at the Colonial Williamsburg Foundation, to identify that table as "the variety known in the period as a center table. By about 1830 such tables were considered indispensable for the properly furnished parlor or drawing room. They were used for taking tea during the day. In the evening they became family gathering centers for sewing, reading, writing, and conversation. At night a sinumbra or other oil lamp was placed in the center of the table for all to share. The table's carved animal paw feet and the turned central shaft suggest a date between the mid-1820s and about 1850. The presence of four feet instead of three points toward a New York origin or something in that vicinity."[3]

On a "page" from another album, a similar "sempstress" sits within the floral bower encircling her elaborately detailed parlor (no. 16). She has put aside her knitting and now holds a pieced quilt block. Across her skirt is written "How much I prize / my Album patch-work / Eliza S. Howell / Dec 24th 1848," an inscription predating that of "the 1th day of January. 1849" that appears on the title page of Lewis Miller's "picturesque album" by only eight days. Her sewing basket, surrounded by the same baroque C-scrolls used by the other artist, sits just beyond the Brussels carpet beneath her feet. On the table beside her, the careful observer will see a small sewing accessory much in favor with early American needleworkers;

15. *Orbis Pictus,* title page

the tiny ink-drawn motif is surely intended to represent a *huswif* (no. 17), a rectangular construction (usually of cotton) that held such small necessities as her needle and thimble, and perhaps an ink-marked ribbon to use as a measuring tape, and which could be rolled up and put into the waist-pockets she might have worn beneath her skirt.

The flowers drawn in such profusion on the annotated pages of Miller's little book were also entered on the "pages" of Eliza's album, floral motifs cut from chintz and appliquéd to a white cotton ground in a technique referred to as *broderie perse*. All but two of the blocks were signed by her family and friends, either with single autographs or with religious references[4] and moral admonitions (no. 18). Beneath two ribbon-tied boughs of leaves, berries, and buds is written "John 6.12 / Gather up / the fragments that remain / that nothing be lost." The signatures and inscriptions on those floral blocks may be Eliza's "gathered fragments," and she has arranged them with admiration and affection within the borders of her patchwork album quilt.

The fringed drapes through which we observe this tableaux are shown held back by a cloak pin, probably of stamped brass or wood,[5] and they are inscribed with verse. On the left,

Friendship

In vain — in different paths we tread —
And though no more mayest soothe or cheer;
Yet we have those hours of friendship shed,
A sweetnefs that still lingers here;
Thy form & look, in memory's glafs,
I still distinctly see;
Thy voice and words, in fancy's ear.
Are whispering still to me.

and on the right,

Eternity

When the dream of life is fled,
When its wasted lamp is dead,
When in cold oblivion's shade,
Beauty, power, & wealth are laid;
Where immortal spirits reign,
There may be all we meet again;
On the tree of life eternal
Man, let all the hope be staid
Which alone, for ever vernal,
Bears a leaf that shall not fade.

Those poems, and the motto hanging within a stenciled frame[6] ("Total / Abstinence / Pledge"), serve coincidentally to identify those three areas that most often inspired the quilts that are the subject of this work: friendship, eternity, and the great social causes addressed during the nineteenth century.

16. The Eliza S. Howell Album Quilt (detail)
Made by Eliza S. Howell
United States. Blocks inscribed Connecticut,
New Brunswick, New York, and Philadelphia
Blocks dated 1846 to 1849
76¾ x 78½ in. (194.9 x 199.4 cm)
Los Angeles County Museum of Art, gift of
William Raymond Graber
Courtesy of Hearts and Hands Media Arts

17. Three *huswifs*
    United States
    Los Angeles County Museum of Art
    Left: circa 1825
        11⅜ x 4¼ in. (28.9 x 10.8 cm)
        American Quilt Research Center Acqui-
        sition Fund

Center: circa 1830
    14 x 3⅝ to 6⅜ in. (35.6 x 9.2 to 16.2 cm)
    American Quilt Research Center Acqui-
    sition Fund
Right: Early nineteenth century
    11⅝ x 3⅛ to 4⅛ in. (29.5 x 7.9 to 10.5 cm)
    Costume Council Fund

NOTES

1. *American Folk Paintings: Paintings and Draw-ings Other Than Portraits from the Abby Aldrich Rockefeller Folk Art Center*. The Abby Aldrich Rockefeller Folk Art Center Series, edited by Beatrix T. Rumford, no. 2. (Boston: Little, Brown, 1988), 134–51.
2. Miller, a bachelor who died ill and impover-ished, had great affection for his brother's four children, and they were often the recipi-ents of handpainted valentines and other small tokens of remembrance. One such senti-mental drawing was sent to his great-niece, Jane Harriet Edie, in Virginia. Illustrated, *American Folk Paintings*, 140.
3. Ronald L. Hurst, curator of furniture, the Colonial Williamsburg Foundation. Letter to author, 5 October 1994.
4. One block is inscribed with Chinese charac-ters to read "Thou art the light of the world." and "Whenever I believe in you, we thank the Lord." The author is grateful to June Li, assis-tant curator, Far Eastern art, Los Angeles County Museum of Art, for this translation.
5. Ronald L. Hurst, letter.
6. Consistent with the period, the frame hangs from an exposed cord, finely drawn to detail its twists and tassels.

18. The Eliza S. Howell Album Quilt (detail)
    Signed Abby Van Duven
    "— Go, fix some weighty truth
    Chain down some pafsion; do some generous
    good;
    Teach ignorance to see, or grief to smile;
    Correct thy friend; befriend thy greatest foe
    Or with warm heart and confidence divine
    Spring up and lay strong hold on him who
    made thee."

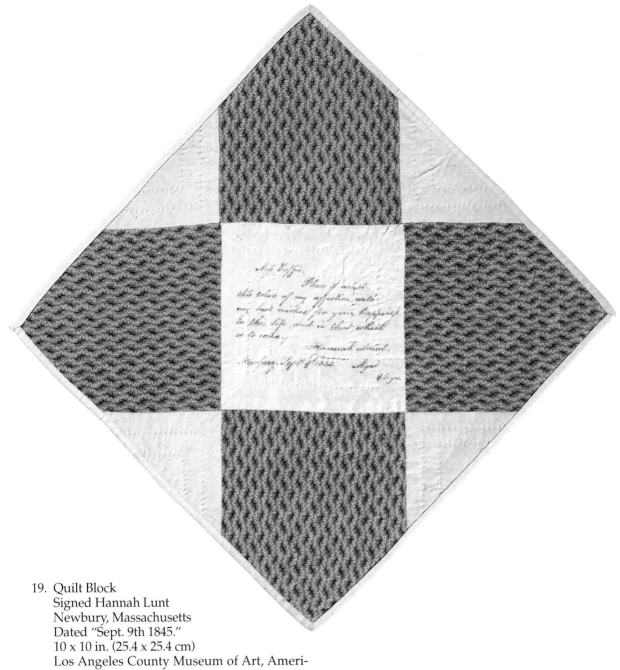

19. Quilt Block
Signed Hannah Lunt
Newbury, Massachusetts
Dated "Sept. 9th 1845."
10 x 10 in. (25.4 x 25.4 cm)
Los Angeles County Museum of Art, American Quilt Research Center Acquisition Fund
"Mifs Coffin, / Please to accept / this token of my affection, with / my best wishes for your happinefs / in this life, and in that which / is to come. / Hannah Lunt / Newbury, Sept / 9th 1845. / Aged/86 yrs."

Please to Accept This Token of My Affection

On 9 September 1845, at age twenty-five, Hannah Woodman Coffin, the privileged daughter of Capt. Nathaniel and Hannah Moody (Woodman) Coffin of Newbury, Massachusetts, married Charles Woodman ("Age 23, merchant of Dover, N.H.").[1] It was on that day that Hannah Lunt, in her eighty-sixth year, inscribed a friendship block (no. 19) to that younger Hannah. Retaining the script of her younger days, Mrs. Lunt used a "long s," substituting "f" for a first "s" in correctly addressing Hannah as *Mifs* Coffin; Hannah had a younger sister and as late as 1884, *Dorcas Magazine* responded to an inquiry from one of its readers, "Young Lady (Bloomfield) — If you are the eldest of the girls in your family, you are Miss Smith, and your sisters Miss Ella and Miss Fannie. After your marriage the next sister becomes Miss Smith."[2]

Mrs. Lunt's block joined twenty-seven others; only two are unsigned and most bear dates both shortly prior to and shortly after the marriage. The signatures on these blocks confirm the close but often complex kinships through which the participants in this fashionable undertaking were bound. Of the twelve cotton prints and plaids from which the pieced blocks were worked (no. 20),

seven were in the same purple print selected by (or assigned to) Mrs. Lunt, and they are signed by the bride's aunts (her mother's sisters), Aunt Jane Woodman, Aunt Abby, and Aunt Edna Maria (the latter two never married), and by her cousin Sophronia; it was also the fabric used by three of Aunt Elizabeth's cousins by marriage, three sisters who also shared a contemporary preference for a floral theme in their selection of verse:

I'll pull a bunch of buds and flowers, /
And tie a ribbond round them. / If
you'll but think in your lonely hours, /
Of your own little girl that bound them.
S. [Sarah] L. Disney

I would bring to thee a cowslip / My
beautiful my own,
Such a fair and modest flower / Is like
to thee alone.
E. [Elizabeth] J. Disney

There is a flower that oft unheeded
grows, / Amid the splendor of the summer's ray, / And though this little
flower no sweets disclose / Yet it will
tell thee all I wish to say. / Forget me
not /Mary E. Disney

21. Charles Balthazar Saint Memin
Virginia, early nineteenth century
Portrait of Elizabeth McClung Wickham
Charcoal drawing on paper with pink wash
22 x 15½ in. (55.9 x 39.4 cm)
Courtesy of the Museum of Early Southern
Decorative Arts

20. Details of the textiles used in the Newbury
quilt blocks made for presentation to Hannah
Coffin by her family and friends in 1845.
(Below and pages 23 and 24)

Cousin Elizabeth recalled their friendship: "Forget me not around your hearth, / When clearly shines the ruddy stone, / For dear hath been its hour of mirth / To me, sweet friend! in older days."

These particular verses are similar in both style and sentiment to those suggested by such a source as *Godey's Lady's Book and Magazine* for inscription in the autograph albums that had enjoyed great popularity since the 1830s. Others allude specifically to the occasion that prompted the giving of the blocks: Cousin Almira Johnson referred to "Domestic happiness, thou only bliss/Of Paradise that has survived the fall!" and [Aunt?] Elizabeth wrote, "I saw two clouds at morning,/Tinged with the rising sun;/And in the dawn they floated on/and mingled into one." Almost two months after Hannah's marriage, cousin S. [Sarah] M. [Mulliken] Stone wrote, "Whate'er I could wish thee is already thine."

In addition to the use of dress fabrics fashionable to the period, the same techniques of construction applied to clothing were in many instances applied to America's quilts. The same elements of finishing, and such embellishment as handwoven tape binding, piping, and bits of soutache braid, are particularly in evidence. On these Newbury blocks, the pattern chosen to contain

a. Block signed by D. C. Marsh. (left)
b. Block signed by S. B. Coffin. (right)

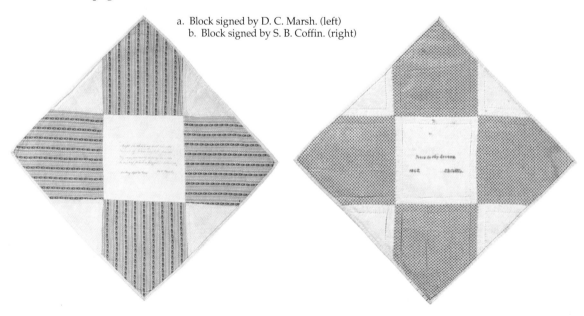

c. Used in blocks signed by Sophronia E. Coffin, E. J. Disney, Mary E. Disney, S. L. Disney, Hannah Lunt, Abby Woodman, E. M. Woodman, and Jane Woodman. (left)

d. Used in blocks signed by E. J. Noyes and Sarah J. Noyes. (right)

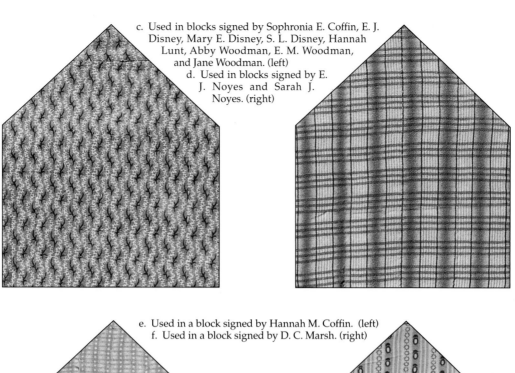

e. Used in a block signed by Hannah M. Coffin. (left)

f. Used in a block signed by D. C. Marsh. (right)

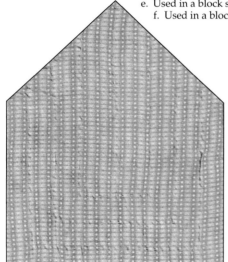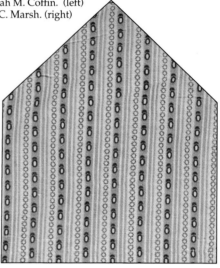

g. Used in a block inscribed but unsigned. (left)

h. Used in a block signed by S. B. Coffin. (right)

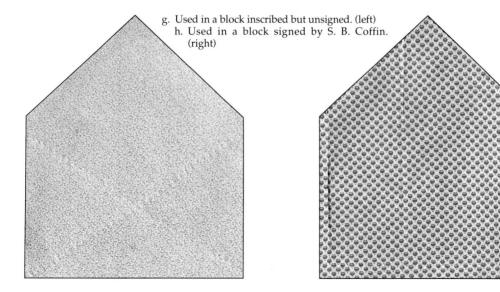

i. Used in a block signed by S. M. Stone and in a
block inscribed but unsigned. (left)
j. Used in a block signed by Sarah Stone.
(right)

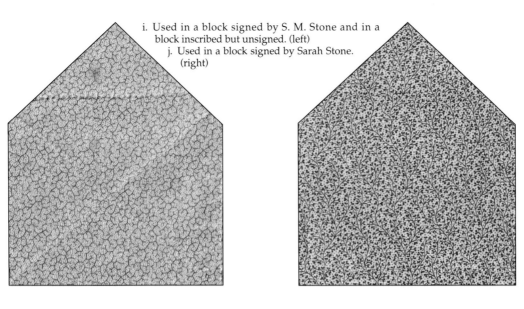

k. Used in blocks signed by Harriet M. Woodman
and Jane E. Woodman. (left)
l. Used in blocks signed by "Elizabeth"
and Caroline Mulliken. (right)

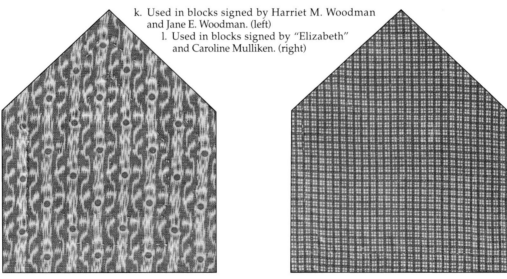

m. Used in blocks signed by Elizabeth D. Lunt and
Miss E. Lunt. (left)
n. Used in blocks signed by Serena Johnson, Almira Johnson, Sarah E. Coffin, and Susan H. Coffin.
(right)

those sentimental verses is itself seen on the sleeve of a dress (no. 21) worn earlier in the century by Elizabeth McClung Wickham, daughter of Dr. James McClung, a member of the Continental Congress, and wife of John Wickham, a Richmond, Virginia, lawyer.

Once pieced and inscribed, each of these individual blocks was then quilted and bound, making the final construction of the quilt a relatively easy task, but Hannah's responsibility nevertheless. She died 3 December 1854, barely nine years after her mother had inscribed on her block, "Let love abide 'till death divide." The blocks were still unjoined.

NOTES

1. *Vital Records of Newbury Massachusetts to the End of the Year 1849,* Vol. II, part 1 (Salem, MA: Essex Institute, 1911), 108. Charles's father was a speaker of the New Hampshire House of Representatives and died shortly after his son was born. (Noreen C. Pramberg, executive secretary, the Sons and Daughters of the First Settlers of Newbury, Massachusetts, letter to the author, 30 March 1992).
2. *Dorcas Magazine* (June 1884): 173.

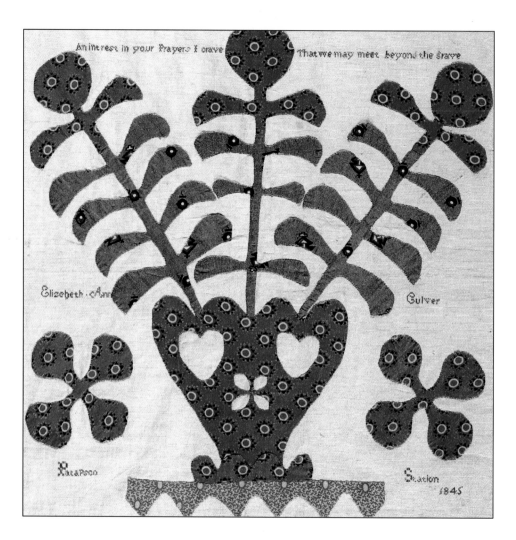

22. The Eggleston Bedcover (detail)
Probably Maryland
Marked 1844, 1845, 1846, and 1847
90 x 90 in. (228.6 x 228.6 cm)
Mr. and Mrs. Thomas H. Morgan
"An interest in your Prayers I crave That we
may meet beyond the grave / Elizabeth Ann
Culver / Patapsco Station 1845"

Scribed and Stenciled, Stamped and Stitched

The Traveling Preachers file in the United Methodist Historical Society (Baltimore Conference)[1] records Reverend William George Eggleston's pastoral appointments between 1837 and 1892; they are recorded also on an appliquéd bedcover whose blocks (no. 22) note locations and dates corresponding to several of Eggleston's circuit assignments[2] during the mid-1840s. (Although oral tradition has held the piece to have been presented to the Reverend Mr. Eggleston, faded writing in the four corners of one anchor-centered block notes "To Mrs. W, G, Eggleston. / March 4, 1847. / Presented by / Mrs. Julia D. Terrett / Washington, D.C."). In their signing, dating, and inscriptions, the blocks are scribed, stenciled, stamped, and stitched, presenting examples of the four principal methods by which nineteenth-century women marked their quilts.

The ink used by Tryphena Ely White to title her 1805 Massachusetts journal (no. 23) and to record the occasions on which "Polly and I went over to Mr. Reed's to quilting"[3] was most probably of her own making, with the same eventually corrosive qualities that at that time made even commercially produced ink generally unsuitable for use on fabric. By at least the mid-1830s, however, products such as Payson's Indelible Ink were widely available for that purpose, and they were used on American quilts throughout the rest of the nineteenth century.

This composition not only requires (excepting in *very thin* cloth) no previous preparation, but it may be used at any time, even in cloudy and damp weather; and as it will not corrode the cloth,[4] it is not necessary to wash this, like other kinds, soon after being used,

23. Title page of Tryphena E. White's journal New York, 1805

27

24. The Eggleston Bedcover (detail)
   "Sarah C. Jones. / Washington City. / January 19th 1847"

25. The Eggleston Bedcover (detail)
   "Susan A. Jenkins / Ellicotts Mills / Md"

26. The Eggleston Bedcover (detail)
   "I love to look at nature pure / I love to dwell on friendship's past, / And think it all forever sure / in one eternal rest at last. / Margaret Dushane / Balt. / 46"

27. The Eggleston Bedcover (detail)
   "Rebecca M. Jones / Washington City / January 19th 1847"

to prevent it from spreading. When first used, the writing will be pale; but by complying with the directions below, it becomes of a deep black, which cannot be effaced, either by washing or time. [from paper label surrounding Payson's Indelible Ink circa 1853]

The writings on several of the Eggleston blocks (nos. 24 and 25) however, suggest Payson's was not used, or instructions were not followed!

The label continues to instruct: "Shake the ink well; then with a quill pen that has not been used on other ink, write what you wish . . . .A new steel pen, or a clean gold one, may be used, if more convenient." During this period, in the marking of their own quilts and the friendship blocks (nos. 26 and 27) being given or exchanged within their circles of families and friends, pen and Payson's Ink became as indispensable to quiltmakers as their needle and thread.

In the middle of the nineteenth century, the ability to write a fine hand joined with the ability to sew a fine seam to produce the elegant signatures and verses that were written in large numbers on the surfaces of friendship and album quilts, and it was a skill taught to young scholars in fashionable schools, many of which were established particularly for that purpose. In the eighteenth century, there was in fact a recognized "Boston Style of Writing" taught by honored writing masters and said to be identifiable in the letters and signatures of that city's scholars, patriots, and clergy,[5] as well as the young women who would one day join their mothers and aunts around a quilting frame securing, perhaps, less power but greater pleasure. In the nineteenth century, fashionable skills once cultivated primarily by the upper class were placed within the means of an expanding, aspiring middle class through women's periodicals and instructional books; with the

28. Illustration, *Spencerian Key to Practical Penmanship*

1848 publication of the Spencerian System of Practical Penmanship, Platte R. Spencer realized his "sublime resolution to rescue from its undeserved obscurity the practical Art of Writing . . . .an idea of graceful lines, and curves, and characters"[6] (nos. 28 and 29). The degree of his success is apparent on American quilts.

The stencils ordered by Martha and Rebecca Carter, and by Annie, Emily, and Francis Tomlinson, have all been used; Francis's has been worn nearly through. Their names had been cut in the tiniest of letters into small metal plates (approximately 2¾ in. wide x 1⅜ in. high), and with only a few pieces of equipment (ink, brush, and a small glass plate), their names and the modest motifs that surrounded them had been transferred onto their clothing and their house-

29. "Spencerian Ladies' Hand.," *Spencerian Key to Practical Penmanship*

30. Stencil Kit with metal plates
Dr. Byron and Sarah Dillow

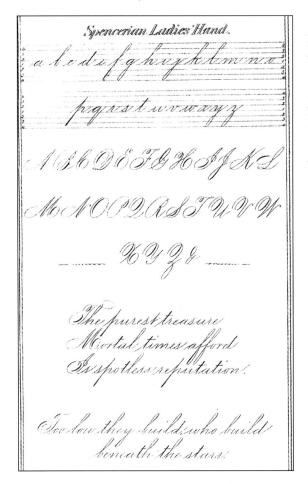

hold linens, and perhaps onto their quilts as well. The plates have all survived together (no. 30) in a box identified within its lid as from W. H. Moll & Bro., Stencil Cutters, Souder's Station, Pennsylvania. Most important, the box top announces its contents to be "Superior Indelible Ink, / For Marking Clothing with Stencil Plates."

DIRECTIONS
Stir the ink well with a stick, pour a small quantity on a piece of / glass, and rub it with the brush until well mixed. Lay the plate on / the article to be marked (which should be cleaned and free from / starch) with only one thickness of cloth between the plate and table; / rub the brush over the name until the letters appear perfectly plain, / then heat the article well from three to five minutes by a fire or with / a hot flat iron.

Clean the brush and plate *after using* with a cloth and turpentine, / rub the plate carefully while lying flat on the

31a. and 31b. Linen markers
David Hewett

table. Should the Ink become *too thick*, add one or two drops of turpentine, and stir together / thoroughly. Cork the vial *closely* after using. *Never use cold water / at the first washing*, but wash in the usual manner with hot water / and soap.

Please follow instructions if you wish the Ink to give satisfaction.

The quiltmaker's name might also be set in moveable type, held within the rectangular opening of a lead linen marker (no. 31a). The face of the marker most often chosen for use on a quilt block was that of two birds kissing, occasionally with two hearts as well (no. 31b), or an eagle whose wings spread across the top of the small device.[7] It was that latter image Sarah Ann Fell pressed onto an inked pad and then onto the surface of her block of "Laurel Leaves" (no. 32).

In the eighteenth and early nineteenth centuries, if a quilt were to be discreetly marked, as with household linens, it would most often be done with small cross-stitched initials, those the quiltmaker had perfected as a young girl on her marking sampler. On the most original of the appliquéd blocks on the Eggleston bedcover, it is that earlier method by which the maker identified herself and her work (nos. 33, 34, 35, 36, 37, and 38).

NOTES

1. Betty Ammons, United Methodist Historical Society, Baltimore Conference. Letter to Mrs. Thomas H. Morgan, 29 July 1994.
2. Baltimore; Brotherton, Anne Arundel County; Ellicotts Mills, Patapsco Station; Springfield, Virginia, and Washington City.
3. Fanny Kellogg, *Tryphena Ely White's Journal, Being a Record, Written One Hundred Years Ago, of the Daily Life of a Young Lady of Puritan Heritage* (New York: Grafton, 1904), 25. In these early journals, the homes to which the ladies go to "quiltings" is usually identified as the husbands', as in "Mr. Reed's."
4. For a technical analysis, the author particularly recommends Margaret T. Ordonez's excellent article "Ink Damage on Nineteenth-Century Cotton Signature Quilts," *Uncoverings* 13 (1992), 148–68.
5. Anna Green Winslow, *Diary of Anna Green Winslow: A Boston School Girl of 1771*. Edited by Alice Morse Earle. (Boston: Houghton, Mifflin, 1894), 92–93.
6. H. C. Spencer, *Spencerian Key to Practical Penmanship* (New York: Ivison, Blakeman, Taylor, 1879), 5.
7. In "Unusual Use of Marking Devices Produces Rarities," *Maine Antique Digest* (September 1993), 18E, David Hewett points out a philatelic application for these devices. Complete with birds and eagles and foliate borders, the linen markers were also occasionally used as a postal origination stamp.

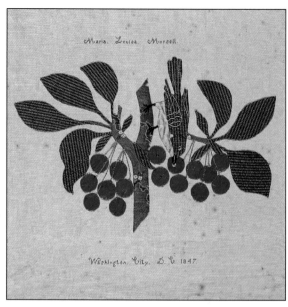

32. The Eggleston Bedcover (detail)
    "Sarah Ann Fell"

33. The Eggleston Bedcover (detail)
    "Maria. Louisa. Mosell. / Washington, City.
    D.C. 1847"

34. The Eggleston Bedcover (detail)
    "Martha E. Baldwin / Brotherton. / A. A.
    County. / M.D."

35. The Eggleston Bedcover (detail)
    "E. A. Isaac."

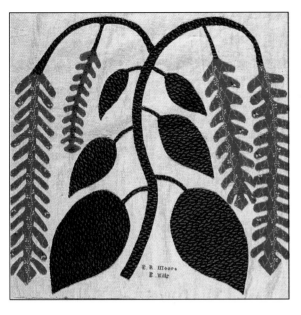

36. The Eggleston Bedcover (detail)
"E. R. Moore / E. Mills"

37. The Eggleston Bedcover (detail)
"Jane Iles / Ellicotts Mills."

38. The Eggleston Bedcover (detail)
"Margt. Iles."

39. The Boardman Presentation Quilt
Made for Reverend and Mrs. George S.
Boardman by the ladies of the Third Presby-
terian Church
Philadelphia, Pennsylvania
Marked 1843
105⅝ x 120½ in. (275.9 x 306.1 cm)
Los Angeles County Museum of Art, pur-
chased with funds provided by the Don Ben-
ito Chapter of the Questers, partial gift of
Dolores B. Thomas

Presented by the Ladies

Floral sprays cut from a significant number of block- and roller-printed cottons were sewn to each of 101 plain white "pages" prepared within the Presbyterian community in Philadelphia in 1843. The squares were signed and bound together in tidy rows around a central medallion that contained the history of the splendid quilt (no. 39) that was the result: "Presented / to the / Revd. George A. & Sarah Boardman / by the Ladies of the / Third Presbyterian Church / of Philadelphia / 1843." (no. 40)

In 1821, after two years of traveling on horseback to preach the gospel in what was then the Far West, in Ohio and Kentucky, Reverend George Boardman was installed in the church at Watertown, New York, to begin a "precious and fruitful pastorate there of sixteen years duration." Following additional pastoral assignments in Rochester, New York, and Columbus, Ohio, he spent a brief year in Philadelphia at the Third Presbyterian Church, more informally referred to as the Old Pine Street Church. His departure in 1843 to take charge of the Second Church at Rome, New York (and thereafter New York pastorates in Cherry Valley, Cazenovia, Ogdensburg, and Little Falls), was marked

40. The Boardman Presentation Quilt (detail)

by the presentation of this magnificent album quilt. Just inside the top curve of the central floral wreath it is further inscribed, "How beautiful upon the mountains are the feet of Him that bringeth good tidings." The Reverend George Boardman's obituary noted that he had always "commended the gospel by his holy walk and beautiful example."[1]

Through an extraordinary number of common threads, one can move seamlessly through a segment of similar friendship album quilts worked together in Philadelphia and in New Jersey during a ten-year span, 1840–50. The workmanship on all is uniformly fine (and not unexpected for it represents the standard to which these ladies would be held by their peers and by themselves), and as a technique, *broderie perse*[2] (no. 41) continued to be a favored method of expressing oneself in the "language of flowers."[3] (On the Boardman quilt, Pamelia Adeline Higerood [?] used a highly glazed cotton floral chintz and in addition to her signature inscribed, "O be each flower a book, where

41. The Boardman Presentation Quilt (detail)

42. The Boardman Presentation Quilt (detail)

we may see / Dear records of Religion and of Thee / And may all nature move / Thoughts of thy matchless love," no. 42).

Among the fabrics, there seems to have been a particular affection for a certain moss rose. The flower itself, once a simple country garden favorite, was moving toward a period of immense popularity that would peak in 1850–60, and its realistic depiction was an art that the most accomplished of young ladies would be expected to master. As an alternative to private instruction, the growing middle class had long turned to a number of instructional books or women's periodicals from which they could develop the upper-class attributes to which they aspired. Nathaniel Whittock's 1829 directions for the drawing and painting of the "Full Blown Moss Rose" was a gentle lesson for its depiction in pencil (no. 43) and watercolors (no. 44) on the pages of the albums of the following decades: "This flower is always acknowledged by poets and painters of all nations to be the peculiar favourite of nature,

43. Illustration from Nathaniel Whittock, *The Art of Drawing and Colouring from Nature, Flowers, Fruit, and Shells* (1829)

44. Illustration from Nathaniel Whittock, *The Art of Drawing and Colouring from Nature, Flowers, Fruit, and Shells* (1829)

and has obtained the title of queen of flowers; it is, therefore, chosen for the concluding lesson in water-colour painting, and it will require all the ability of the student to produce it with brilliancy and freedom. . . . Sufficient directions for the unblown roses, buds, &c. will be found in Lesson VII.; and for the leaves Lesson IV."[4] If the quiltmaker wished

45. The Boardman Presentation Quilt (detail)

46. The Boardman Presentation Quilt (detail)

47. The Sewing Society Quilt
Philadelphia, Pennsylvania
Marked 1846–50
97 x 106 in. (246.4 x 269.2 cm)
Philadelphia Museum of Art, gift of Mrs.
Sterett Ridgely Prevost

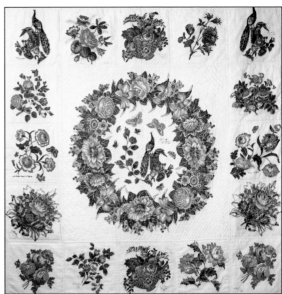

48. The Boardman Presentation Quilt (detail)

49. The Emma Fish Album Quilt (detail)
Made by Emma M. Fish for "Aunt Eliza Moore"
Trenton, New Jersey
Marked 1843
104 x 94 in. (264.2 x 238.8 cm)
DAR Museum, gift of Mrs. C. Edward Murray

also to enter it on her album block, she could do so with less time and with less talent through the artful choice of a brilliant moss rose cut from a floral chintz (no. 45).

In 1852, Sarah Davenport, a young quiltmaker, moved between quilting parties (see p. 7) and drawings lessons: "I have drawn a considerable today, my drawing being on sheets of Bristol Board intened after it is painted for an Album . . . "; "I have drawn in Monochromatic Drawing a little while this morning and then went up to Uncles and took my lesson in Water colors . . . "; "painted all day and I have some pretty peices a painting such as . . . beawkas and wreaths, etc."[5] A wreath-encircled Eliza Howell (see no. 16) had written on her prized album patchwork, "Gather up the fragments that remain that nothing be lost," and although the biblical reference (John 6.12) from which that phrase was drawn was the instruction Jesus had given to his disciples after they had filled themselves with the loaves and the fishes, for Eliza those frag-

ments were surely the memories of tender association with family and friends, and that was perhaps true as well for Eliza J. McCorckle, whose signature was contained on a scroll within an oval open wreath (no. 46) on the Boardman quilt. Although amateur lady botanists pressed flowers for purposes of study and classification, others such as Queen Victoria did so in the fashionable sentimental collection of "mementos of friendship," often in the form of flowers plucked from last night's bouquet or from the wreaths that had decorated the grave of a loved one.[6] Open and closed floral wreaths — cut, constructed, appliquéd, and drawn — were a significant decorative device on these quilts, and they appeared in particular profusion on a quilt (no. 47) probably worked within the Sewing Society of the First Baptist

50. The Sarah Flickwir Album Quilt
     Made by Sarah Flickwir
     Philadelphia, Pennsylvania
     Marked 1840–46
     91½ x 92 in. (232.4 x 233.7 cm)
     Philadelphia Museum of Art, gift of Mrs. F.
     Willard Wood in memory of Mrs. Frank W.
     Wood, née Rebecca Williamson Flickwir

51. Textile
England
1825–30
Courtesy, Winterthur Museum

52a. and 52b. Illustrations from Nathaniel Whittock, *The Art of Drawing and Colouring from Nature, Flowers, Fruit, and Shells* (1829)

Church of Philadelphia.[7] Absolute authorship of this quilt has not been established, but transcription of the verses contained within the larger wreaths indicates they honored or memorialized several of the founding families of that church, and we know there was within this particular sewing society a tradition of album quilts such as that presented in 1846 to Sister Deborah Wade of the Karen Mission in Burma:

> permit me in behalf of the Sisters of the Sewing Society, to present for your acceptance, an Album bedquilt. —

Inscribed on it you will find, when you have leisure to examine it many precious promises from the word of life, and sentiments warm from Christian hearts. Receive it, as it is intended, not, from any value in itself, but as a small token of affection, for the Master's sake, and the high estimation in which you are regarded by us — When our humble names appear before you Pray for us.[8]

Curatorial comments further suggest this particular piece might have been commissioned to raise funds for the continuing needs of the church in both its spiritual and

53. Shells
    Watercolor on wove heavy drawing board
    Probably 1829–40
    7⅞ x 9⅜ in. (20 x 23.3 cm)
    Abby Aldrich Rockefeller Folk Art Center,
    Williamsburg, Virginia

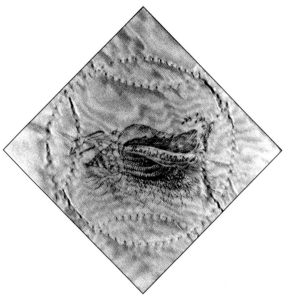

54. The Quaker Silk Quilt (detail)
    Pennsylvania and New Jersey
    Circa 1850
    118 x 132½ in. (299.7 x 336.6 cm)
    Los Angeles County Museum of Art, Costume Council Fund

social outreach; signatures on similar squares were sometimes those of the sponsor of that particular block, rather than that of the needlewoman herself.

The peacock perched on a flower-based pedestal near the top left corner of the Sewing Society quilt is a second chintz motif that was used in substantial numbers. It anchored the corners of the row of blocks surrounding the flower-filled urn on the Boardman quilt (no. 48); it was placed in the center of a friendship album quilt made for "Aunt Eliza Moore, Trenton, N.J., March 4, 1843" (no. 49); and on Sarah Flickwir's Philadelphia quilt (no. 50) it appeared with almost a dozen different chintz birds, and with the same moss roses with which it appeared beneath the Boardman dedication (see no. 48).[9]

Among the cut-chintz blocks on the herringbone-quilted surface of the Flickwir quilt are a series of seashells, a motif appearing through all the decorative arts of the period.

In her New England girlhood home, Lucy Larcom remembered that

> Mantel-pieces were adorned with nautilus and conch-shells, and with branches and fans of coral; and children had foreign curiosities and treasures of the sea for playthings. There was one imported shell that we did not value much, it was so abundant — the freckled univalve they called a "prop." Yet it had a mysterious interest for us little ones. We held it to our ears, and listened for the sound of the waves, which we were told that it still kept, and always would keep. I remember the time when I thought that the ocean was really imprisoned somewhere within that narrow aperture.[10]

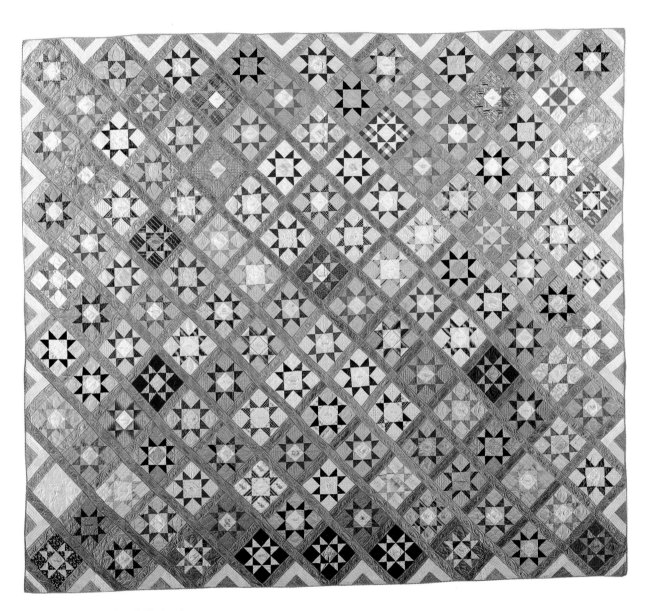

55. The Quaker Silk Quilt

Shells placed amid coral and seaweed were the subject of a number of printed cottons, including one roller-printed in sepia with yellow added by a surface roller (no. 51); Nathaniel Whittock included instructions for "drawing and colouring" them (nos. 52a and 52b), one of which (no. 52a) was the print source for a small watercolor (no. 53) by an unidentified artist; and in 1852, Sarah Davenport, "a drawing and painting nearly all day under Cousin Frances's guidance," added to her youthful repertoire of leaves and "beawkas and wreaths" another motif: "several shells with sea weeds all around

56. The Quaker Silk Quilt (detail)

57. The Quaker Silk Quilt (detail)

58. The Quaker Silk Quilt (detail)

59. The Quaker Silk Quilt (detail)

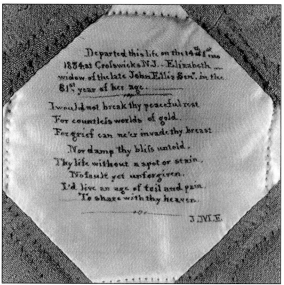

60. The Charlotte Gillingham Album Quilt
Attributed to Charlotte Gillingham
Made for Samuel Padgett Hancock
Philadelphia, Pennsylvania
Marked 1842–43
97 x 126 in. (246.4 x 320 cm)
Philadelphia Museum of Art, gift of the five
granddaughters of Samuel Padgett Hancock:
Mrs. Levis Lloyd Mann, Mrs. H. Maxwell
Langdon, Mrs. George K. Helbert, Mrs. Nelson
D. Warwick, and Mrs. Granville B. Hopkins

61. The Mary P. Allen Album Quilt
Made by Mary P. Allen
Pennsylvania and New Jersey
Marked 1841–47
89 x 117 in. (226.1 x 297.2 cm)
Los Angeles County Museum of Art, gift of
Pam Ferris

62. The Mary Allen Quilt (detail)

63. The Mary Allen Quilt (detail)

it."[11] The image (no. 54) found its small subtle way onto a magnificent Quaker pieced silk quilt (no. 55), as did the open spray (no. 56) and birds (no. 57) earlier worked in bright glazed chintz; the ink-drawn birds and floral sprays also embellish a series of such mourning symbols as the funerary urn (no. 58) inscribed "In / Memory / of / Deborah Bunting / The memory of the / Just is blessed." As did the Philadelphia Sewing Society quilt, this quilt bears a significant number of mourning verses, noting departures and honoring virtues (no. 59).

The images on another Quaker quilt (no. 60) are in stark contrast to the aesthetic simplicity we more often associate with this religious society. But even among this dazzling array of complex pieced and appliquéd blocks, the creative components we have identified as common to this particular group of quilts are present: sprays of chintz flowers create the outer border and embellish the blocks, for example, and open and closed wreaths encircle inked birds and floral sprays. The quilt is assumed to have been made as a wedding present for Samuel Padgett Hancock by his fiancée, Charlotte Gillingham, whom he married on 22 February 1844, and it has been suggested that the construction of the blocks was her work alone.[12] Each of those tender tokens was signed and dated by friends and by members of their extended families, and among those names are at least twenty (including those of Samuel and Charlotte) that appear on another quilt of similar shape (no. 61), both having been cut for a four-poster bedstead.[13] As on the Quaker silk quilt, the recurring motifs binding these quilts together are

64. The Mary Allen Quilt (detail)

65. The Mary Allen Quilt (detail)

discreetly entered as small sketches, although predominantly red-printed calicoes and white muslin were the stuff of which this quilt was made. Mourning symbols appear (no. 62) as does a mourning verse, the latter in the principal block within a delicate inked floral spray, and all contained within a pieced and appliquéd floral wreath (no. 63):

> 10th Mo 1847 —
> Mary P Allen
> I will not mourn my griefs below
> Nor all their baneful train
> But hope at last to meet above
> My early Friends again

There is an abundance of intricate drawings on this quilt, including boats and buildings (no. 64). On one small sketch is inscribed "Hannah Hilliard / Cousin" (no. 65). Such specifics of kinship are often included with the signatures on these quilts, and on Samuel Hancock's quilt, a block is signed "From thy cousin / Mary P Allen." Hannah Hilliard was a cousin to both.

Technical and stylistic preferences provide a rich resource for establishing the regional characteristics of these Delaware Valley quilts, but it is in the inscriptions on their surfaces that their purpose is most simply stated. From between the bright blocks on Mary Allen's quilt, for example: "When 'neath this quilt thy form reclines / Please think of him who penned these lines."

NOTES

1. For the facts of Reverend George Boardman's private and pastoral life, and for information on the women who signed the blocks on his quilt, I am indebted to Glenna Merrill in Brigham City, Utah, who worked extensively on my behalf in church and census records. Mrs. Merrill's genealogical research assistance extended also to those named on the Spiritualists quilt (pp. 130–32).

2. "She cut squares of white, about a foot square, and in the centre of those, she sewed down bunches of flowers, cut out very neatly from the high colored furniture chintz . . . .and the effect was very beautiful." Florence Hartley, *The Ladies' Hand Book of Fancy and Ornamental Work* (Philadelphia: J. W. Bradley, 1861), 193.

3. The expression of sentiment through flowers drew heavily on the Romanticism of the previous century and was intensified through such French publications as *Le Language des fleures* (Charlotte de Latour, 1833) and their subsequent translation and imitation. Nicolette Scourse, *The Victorians and their Flowers* (London: Croom Helm, 1983), 10.

4. Nathaniel Whittock, *The Art of Drawing and Colouring from Nature, Flowers, Fruit, and Shells; To Which Is Added, Correct Directions for Preparing the Most Brilliant Colours for Painting on Velvet, with the Mode of Using Them; Also, the New Method of Oriental Tinting* (London: Isaac Taylor Hinton, 1829), Lesson XVIII.

5. Sarah Davenport, "The Journal of Sarah Davenport: May 1, 1849 through May 16, 1852," *New Canaan Historical Society Annual* 2 (1950), 86–88.

6. Scourse, *The Victorians and Their Flowers*, 10.

7. The historical information on this quilt has been drawn from its extensive catalogue entry in the *Philadelphia Museum of Art Bulletin* that served as an exhibition catalogue for "As Pieces Here to Pieces Join: American Appliqué Quilts, 1800–1900." Dilys Blum and Jack L. Lindsey, "Nineteenth-Century Appliqué Quilts," *Philadelphia Museum of Art Bulletin* 85, nos. 363/364 (Fall 1989): 28.

8. "Minutes of the Female Missionary Society of the First Baptist Church of Philadelphia" (collection of the church). Ibid.

9. Two of these peacock motifs, and two of the same large brown leaves that appear on the Flickwir quilt, are also appliquéd onto the blocks of an individually made album quilt inscribed "Anna E. W. Sterling, Trenton, New Jersey, 1844." Illustrated in Nancy and Donald Roan, *Lest I Shall Be Forgotten* (Green Lane, PA: Goschenhoppen Historians, 1993), 45.

10. Lucy Larcom, *A New England Girlhood: Outlined from Memory* (Boston: Houghton, Mifflin, 1892), 94.

11. Davenport, "Journal," 86.

12. Jessica F. Nicoll, *Quilted for Friends: Delaware Valley Signature Quilts, 1840–1855* (Winterthur, DE: Winterthur Museum, 1986), 30.

13. Eighteen of the names appearing on the quilt Charlotte made for Samuel Hancock appear also on the friendship quilt of his cousin, Mary Jane Pancoast (Illustrated, Nicoll, *Quilted for Friends*, 8).

66. The Baltimore Album Quilt
Baltimore, Maryland
Circa 1850
101¼ x 103¼ in. (257.2 x 263.2 cm)
Courtesy Hirschl & Adler, New York

Baltimore's Own

The first half of the nineteenth century had brought the American quiltmaker to the height of her creative moment. Her technical proficiency now intersected with the floral sentimentality that characterized so much of the Victorian aesthetic. The immense popularity of the floral images that were painted and pasted on the pages of albums was surely a principal influence on the increas- ingly imaginative and more fully developed floral images on American album quilts. Even when those floral elements cut from cotton chintz were most artfully arranged into garlands and wreaths, there was a certain creative restraint imposed on the quiltmakers who created the splendid *broderie perse* quilts and bedcovers of the mid-Atlantic states. The floral designs that appeared on the Reverend George Boardman's quilt, for example, were equally the creative vision of those who designed and printed the fabric itself. These preprinted flowers were now joined and eventually overwhelmed by blossoms and leaves and

67. *View of Baltimore, Md. From Federal Hill*
Edwin Whitefield
1847
Lithograph
17⅞ x 40¾ in.
Courtesy Sotheby's, Inc., New York City

68. The Lieutenant-Colonel Watson Memorial
    Quilt
    Baltimore, Maryland
    Circa 1848
    82 x 108 in. (208.3 x 274.3 cm)
    Los Angeles County Museum of Art, Cos-
    tume Council Fund

buds more fully of the quiltmaker's own invention, cut to her liking, layered and overlapped, and embroidered and padded, and gloriously her own. Between 1846 and 1852, these new botanical images came to full flower on a remarkable group of album quilts in Baltimore, Maryland, in one instance (no. 66) encircling the Queen of May herself.[1] The flowers formed the familiar wreaths and sprays, were arranged in baskets and epergnes, and tumbled from cornucopias; they joined other appliquéd blocks depicting public buildings, pastoral scenes, and patriotic images, and the resulting album quilts were sufficiently splendid to affix that city's name to the group as a whole. Baltimore album quilts were shaped and stitched out of the extraordinary imported and domestic textiles available to the ladies in that prosperous port town (no. 67). In discussing "The Advantages of Baltimore as a Trade Centre," a nineteenth-century historian placed particular emphasis on fabrics and fashions:

> And probably in no place outside of the family circle is [refinement] seen to better advantage than in the tastes of [Baltimore] society in dress and fashion. Those *outre* costumes and the strange discord of colors so painfully evident as one travels west of the Alleghany Mountains have no place here.[2]

There is indeed a "refinement" and sophistication seen on the quilts those fashionable

70. Elizabeth Bennett's Quilt (detail)
Baltimore, Maryland
Circa 1840–45
108½ x 111½ in. (275.6 x 283.2 cm)
Museum of Early Southern Decorative Arts

69. The Lieutenant-Colonel Watson Memorial
Quilt (detail)
Signed Mary Harrington

71. The Lieutenant-Colonel Watson Memorial
    Quilt (detail)
    Signed Mary A. Ellis

72. The Lieutenant-Colonel Watson Memorial
    Quilt (detail)
    Signed Marian G. McCormick

ladies worked, achieved in great measure through the tasteful textiles from which their dresses were cut. Although the quilts incorporated the occasional bit of silk or wool, and a particular solid-red twill-weave cotton proved useful, it was a group of primarily printed tabby-weave cottons found to be most adaptable to the quiltmaker's visions. These were so often used that many are easily identified on the most classic of these pieces, especially those on which colors graduate in intensity, often referred to by their French designations of *fondu* (to dissolve, or to melt) or *ombre*, in reference to their shaded qualities.

We know that most of these quilts were made for others, often a minister, but we have little knowledge of the procedural aspects of these particular group-given quilts. Once the contributed squares were assembled, the completed quilt often approached or exceeded 100 inches. The blocks were usually simply joined together with or without sashing, occasionally bordered with meandering floral vines, or with whole cloth such as the popular red, black, and gold acanthus scroll that borders one of the most exceptional of these quilts (see no. 66) and from which segments were sometimes cut to form vases and urns. In a piece such as this, although individual blocks show individual work, it is often difficult to determine whether the actual quilting is the work of one hand or many because the quality of workmanship in that aspect would be expected to be of an even and similar quality. That work may, in fact, have fallen to a professional quilter. Aesthetic decisions on the final surface design may have emerged from a group discussion, but one must wonder whose suggestion it was that at least one (no. 68) should be set, sashed, and bordered with more than 1,700 red and white Flying Geese! (no. 69) That was perhaps a regional influ-

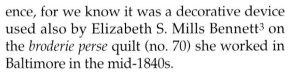

73. The Lieutenant-Colonel Watson Memorial
Quilt (detail)
Signed M. L. Pendergast

74. The Lieutenant-Colonel Watson Memorial
Quilt (detail)
Inscribed "To the Memory of / Col W. H.
Watson"

75. The Major Samuel Ringgold Memorial Quilt
(detail)

ence, for we know it was a decorative device used also by Elizabeth S. Mills Bennett[3] on the *broderie perse* quilt (no. 70) she worked in Baltimore in the mid-1840s.

The floral "pages" of this particular album are signed by Mary A. Ellis (no. 71), Mary Harrington (see no. 69), Amelia Magee, Marian G. McCormick (no. 72), Mrs. E. Eugenia Murphy, M. L. Pendergast (no. 73), Caroline Sheppard, and Sarah R. M. Slicer, but this quilt's most significant block (no. 74) is placed mid-center in the top row, a flag-bedecked monument inscribed "To the Memory of / Col W. H. Watson."[4] Its design is almost identical, if less elaborate in execution, to a square worked in memory of Maj. Samuel Ringgold (no. 75) on which four ruched roses replace the simpler floral shapes more standard to this particular block. The eagle above the inscribed "Ringgold" was used on at least one other,[5] but here the inscription is additionally embellished with crossed flags and standards, and "Ringgold" is outlined with cut steel beads. These blocks and a handful of others (identical in design and often constructed in part of identical fabrics) honored two of Baltimore's most mourned military heroes (nos. 76 and 77), casualties in the immensely unpopular Mexican War. The depicted monument has been identified as a temporary one built in the Merchants Exchange Building where Major Ringgold lay in state in December 1846.[6] News of his death in Palo Alto[7] had reached Baltimore just as volunteers were being organized to join Gen. Zachary Taylor's army in Monterey, and the resulting batallion was placed under the command of William H. Watson. Newly commissioned, Watson had been

admitted to the bar at twenty-one, was elected to the city council at twenty-eight, served in the Maryland House of Delegates at thirty, was elected its speaker at thirty-five, and was shot dead at thirty-eight while leading "Baltimore's Own" in a charge near Monterey.[8] Most of the names on the classic Baltimore album quilts can be traced to the sphere of Baltimore Methodism; Watson was a Methodist as was his mother, Rebecca, and another block in his memory appears on a quilt made for Samuel Williams, a Methodist lay minister, on which a funerary urn is surrounded by a laurel wreath bearing the appliquéd letters W A T S O N.[9] But other areas of association were present in Baltimore and present on these quilts, acknowledged on a few blocks that carry symbols of fraternal organizations, particularly those of the Inde-

76. Lieut. Col. W. H. Watson, illustration from J. Thomas Scharf, *History of Baltimore City and County*

77. Maj. S. Ringgold, illustration from J. Thomas Scharf, *History of Baltimore City and County*

78. The Lieutenant-Colonel Watson Memorial
Quilt (detail)

79. Cornucopia
Wood; red, yellow, and green paint
Guernsey County, Ohio
Length 21 in.
Property of Colwill-McGehee, Baltimore

pendent Order of Odd Fellows, founded there in 1819.[10] Watson was a member.

Masonic symbols such as the square and compass were present as well, on Sophia Beard's quilt[11] for example. The fruit- and flower-filled cornucopia (no. 78) that was among the principal motifs on Baltimore album quilts was drawn from the vocabulary of design that quiltmakers shared with other artisans of the period; it was, for example, also carved in wood, painted in red, yellow, and green, and used in the Cambridge, Ohio, 1007 Masonic Lodge in Guernsey County (no. 79). And according to oral tradition, Henry Smith Lankford (1823–1905) purchased a set of quilt blocks at a Masonic meeting in Baltimore about 1850;[12] they included the ruched and beaded block in memory of Major Ringgold (see no. 75), and they were assembled and quilted (no. 80) by Mr. Lankford's sister, Sarah Anne Whittington Lankford, whose cross-stitched initials were added inside a wreath of apples.

The elusive authorship of individual Baltimore blocks, and of the quilts themselves, continues as a subject of ongoing research and spirited discourse. The Lankford purchase underlines the difficulty in determining whether or not a block was designed and/or made by the woman who signed it. As early as 1946, publishing his early research on Baltimore album quilts, Dr. William Rush Dunton Jr. wrote, "I am of the opinion that [some of] these designs were probably sold at shops or that they are the work of one woman who practiced quilt making as a profession."[13] A recent discovery in the 1850s diary of a young Baltimore Quaker, Hannah Mary Trimble, would seem to confirm that to be the case: following a description of what is surely one of these masterworks, Hannah records her visit to "Mrs. Simon's in Chestnut St. The lady who cut & basted these handsome quilts — saw some pretty squares."[14]

80. The Major Samuel Ringgold Memorial Quilt
Marked "S.A.W.L."
Assembly and quilting attributed to Sarah
Anne Whittington Lankford
Baltimore, Maryland
Circa 1850
99 x 84 in. (213.4 x 251.5 cm)
Abby Aldrich Rockefeller Folk Art Center,
Williamsburg, Virginia

81. The Lieutenant-Colonel Watson Memorial Quilt (detail)

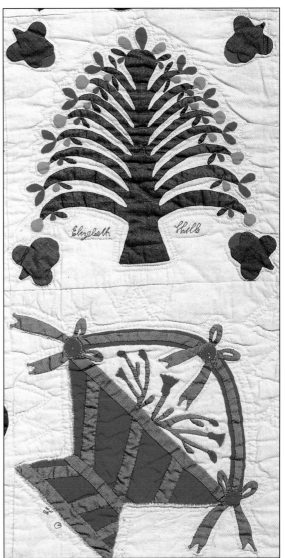

82. The Baskets Quilt (detail)

Other appliquéd album quilts were being worked together during this same period, in Baltimore and elsewhere, perhaps inspired by but independent of those elegant undertakings. These were often presented with a stylistic clarity that might have seemed intolerable to the Baltimore ladies. The greatly admired Baltimore birds (their tail feathers often accentuated with colors exposed by a deft use of reverse appliqué) pose on delicately bending boughs with diverse leaves and berries; they are placed within an intricately assembled floral wreath[15] often tied with a rich blue bow (no. 81). Among the images on a simpler quilt of many baskets (nos. 82 and 83), the bird (no. 84) appears with a fanciful frugality. Both bring honor to the quiltmaker and to her craft.

NOTES

1. Dena S. Katzenberg's *Baltimore Album Quilts,* Exhibition Catalogue (Baltimore: Baltimore Museum of Art, 1981) remains the standard reference in the field. Much is owed to William Rush Dunton Jr., M.D., whose privately published *Old Quilts* (1946) documented his seminal research on this fascinating body of work.

2. J. Thomas Scharf, *History of Baltimore City and County* (Philadelphia: Louis H. Everts, 1881), 285.

3. Elizabeth Mills Bennett was born in 1805, the daughter of Samuel and Rachel Vore Mills. She married John Jones Bennett in Baltimore

83. The Baskets Quilt
    Circa 1850
    87½ x 71¼ in. (222.3 x 181 cm)
    Dr. Byron and Sara Dillow

84. The Baskets Quilt (detail)
    Signed Sarah Jones [?] (top) and Maria Odell
    (bottom)

on 3 November 1825 and died there 15 January 1891. MESDA catalogue of Early Southern Decorative Arts.

4. An additional name, Thomas Bennet, appears to the left of the monument.

5. Illustrated in Katzenberg, *Baltimore Album Quilts,* p. 37.
6. Baltimore *American,* December 17–22, 1846. Cited in Jennifer F. Goldsborough, "Baltimore Album Quilts," *The Magazine Antiques,* (March 1994): 419. I had been aware of ten of these very identifiable blocks on quilts in both public and private collections; Ms. Goldsborough's article illustrates yet another (415).
7. Depictions of Major Ringgold, mortally wounded, were a popular subject. One lithograph, signed in the stone EWC and published in 1846 by J. Baillie, New York, is illustrated in *The Old Print Showcase* 7, no. 1 (January–February 1980): 8.
8. Scharf, *History of Baltimore City and County,* Chapter XIV.
9. Illustrated in Katzenberg, *Baltimore Album Quilts,* opp. p. 88.
10. Ritual emblems of the I. O. O. F. (including the all-seeing eye, the heart on hand, beehive, tent, hourglass, axe, scales, etc.) appear on two quilts illustrated in Katzenberg, *Baltimore Album Quilts,* #23 and #24.
11. Illustrated in Dunton, *Old Quilts,* 118.
12. Object file, Abby Aldrich Rockefeller Folk Art Center.
13. Dunton, *Old Quilts,* 119.
14. Quoted in Goldsborough, *Baltimore Album Quilts,* 419. The diary is in the manuscripts division of the Library of Maryland History at the Maryland Historical Society. Additional excerpts and interpretive text are included in this important article.
15. See no. 66, block 2D, and no. 80, block 3A.

85. The Oak Leaf and Reel Quilt
    Made for Albert F. Guthrie
    Bucks County, Pennsylvania
    Circa 1845–50
    104 x 104 in. (264.2 x 264.2 cm)
    Los Angeles County Museum of Art, gift of
    the Betty Horton Collection

$\mathcal{I}\,\mathcal{L}ay\,\mathcal{M}y\,\mathcal{B}ody\,\mathcal{D}own\,to\,\mathcal{S}leep$

$\mathcal{I}$n 1684, a part of the first major German migration into Pennsylvania, Daniel Pastorius wrote to his parents, "I heartily wish for a dozen sturdy Tyrolese to fell the mighty oaks, for whichever way one turns it is *Itur in antiquam sylvam*, everything is forest."[1] A century and a half later, those great stands of oak were stylistically transplanted to cotton quilts and bedcovers in the form of an appliquéd pattern that became an American classic. In Bucks County, Pennsylvania, in the red and green printed cottons so popular in that period and place, twenty-five blocks of Oak Leaf and Reel were signed, set together, surrounded by a swag border, quilted, and presented to Albert F. Guthrie (no. 85), to whom each block is specifically inscribed (no. 86). Although oral tradition has held that he was a minister, "Reverend" does not appear on the quilt.

Acorns and oak leaves were boldly rendered in multiple appliquéd variations (no. 87), quilted on borders, and delicately illustrated in pen and ink in the botanical illustrations that found fertile ground on friendship quilts. They were included on a Quaker quilt top whose tender history[2] suggests how these objects were "quilted together" although apart. During a two-year illness,

Eliza Naudain Corbit (barely thirty years old and living in Cantwell's Bridge, Delaware, with her husband Daniel and their five children) pieced eighty-one quilt blocks. These were then distributed to family and friends for signatures (nine as far away as Galena,

86. The Oak Leaf and Reel Quilt (detail)
"Martha Michener / To / Albert F. Guthrie"

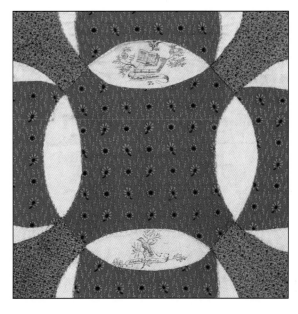

87. The Eggleston Bedcover (detail)
    "E. A. Hughes"

88. Quilt block
    Cantwell's Bridge, Delaware
    Marked 1844
    Courtesy, Winterthur Museum

Illinois), returned to her, sashed, and set together. Although the small branches of the floral spray in the middle of the center block (no. 88) support the signature of Harriet Corbit, the surrounding numbered verses seem to be in another's hand, probably Eliza's own:

> 1st
> Thus far the Lord hath led me on,
> Thus far his power prolongs my days,
> And every evening shall make known
> Some fresh memorial of his grace.
> 1844
>
> 2nd
> Much of my time has run to waste,
> And I perhaps are near my home:
> But he forgives my follies past,
> And gives me strength for days to come.
>
> 3rd
> I lay my body down to sleep,
> Peace is the pillow for my head;

> While well-appointed angels keep
> Their watchful stations round my bed.
>
> 4th
> Thus when the night of death shall come
> My flesh shall rest beneath the ground
> And wait the voice to rouse my tomb,
> With sweet salvation in the sound.

She did not live to see her work put on the frame, for the "night of death" came for Eliza that same year, 1844.

Oak leaves appeared in fragmented form on the border of a Massachusetts summer spread (no. 89). It was a single quiltmaker who worked its central field, ambitiously assuming the challenge of stitching down the slender points of the sunbursts that center each of the nine large blocks, and it must have been her decision that the border should be constructed of appliquéd blocks

89. The Serpent and Dove Bedcover
Probably Massachusetts
Marked 1857
92¼ x 107½ in. (234.3 x 263.1 cm)
Pilgrim/Roy

cut in half (no. 90) although already signed and sketched by others. Reconstructing in our minds that which was cut, we know that in the year 1857 Margeret McMurry, Matilda Miller, "Catherine," Elizabeth Story, Amanda Nelson ("April. 1857. / Amanda Nelson / Why then so unwilling to part / Since there we shall meet again / Engraved on Emmanuels [heart] / At distance we cannot remain."), G. W. Cox ("Absent but remembered."), and M. S. Cox were in some way joined together for a common purpose. The most intricate and symbolic block is one on which the serpent entwines itself among branches held by red calico doves (no. 91). Flowing ribbons advise, "Be ye wise as serpents / and harmless as doves." Two other ink-drawn doves hold an olive branch and a ribbon bearing the name of John McClintock, and between appliquéd and inked birds is a biblical quotation, "How beautiful are the feet of them that preach the gospel of peace and bring glad tidings of good things. Rom 10.15." That those intricate patterns, fine

90. The Serpent and Dove Bedcover, schematic

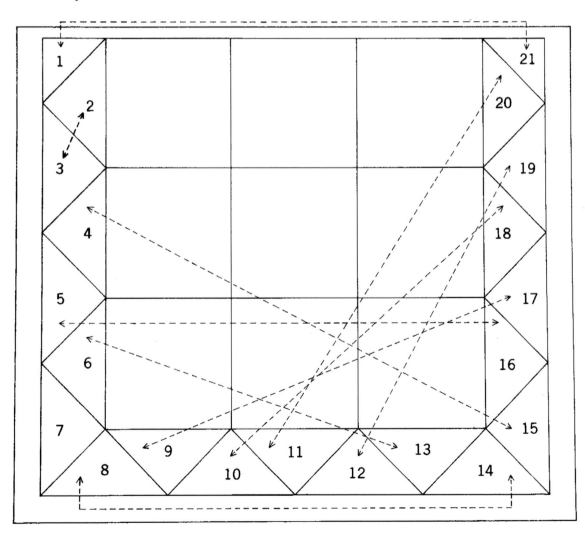

91. The Serpent and Dove Bedcover (detail)

stitching, tender messages, and pious thoughts should have been irrevocably severed seems inexplicable, but it was a choice not unique to this piece. The intent of the messages and the extent of the friendship were occasionally sacrificed in an aesthetic response to color and cloth.

Another bird fell prey to that cruel cut (no. 92). A bird on a leafy branch above an egg-filled nest was a familiar inked vignette on friendship blocks; Matilda Miller's sketch, for example, is similar to that signed by Anna Maria Valentine (no. 93) on Albert F. Guthrie's quilt. Other birds were a primary device for the paper presentation of signatures and short phrases: they perched on delicate flowing ribbons (no. 94) and held the ribbons in their beaks (no. 95). They were the

92. The Serpent and Dove Bedcover (detail)

93. The Oak Leaf and Reel Quilt (detail)

94.   Illustration, *Ornithautographic Album*, 1875

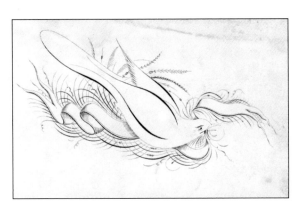

96.   Cover and title page, *Ornithautographic Album*, 1875

95.   Illustration, *Ornithautographic Album*, 1875

images found in an illustrated autograph book (no. 96), and on a calligraphic drawing presented with "compliments to Barcom Diggs" (no. 97).

NOTES

1. Quoted in Beatrice B. Garvan and Charles F. Hummel, *The Pennsylvania Germans: A Celebration of Their Arts 1683–1850* (Philadelphia: Philadelphia Museum of Art, 1982), 37. Pastorius was the Pennsylvania agent for the Frankfort Land Company.
2. Jessica F. Nicoll, *Quilted for Friends: Delaware Valley Signature Quilts 1840–1855* (Winterthur, DE: The Henry Francis Du Pont Winterthur Museum, 1986), 12–13. A drawing of Eliza Corbit is illustrated (Fig. 10) in this very informative exhibition catalogue.

97. Calligraphic drawing
   Compliment to Barcom Diggs
   Ink on paper
   8⅛ x 9⅝ in. (20.6 x 24.5 cm)
   Private Collection

98. Mother's Quilt Top (detail)
United States
Mid-nineteenth century
91¾ x 79¼ in. (233.1 x 201.3 cm)
Darwin D. Bearley Antiques, Akron, Ohio

Mother

Within an extravagant appliquéd floral wreath (no. 98), two simpler sprays form the suggestion of a cartouche, similar in nature to those stamped or sketched in ink on blocks of much smaller dimension. The name embroidered above the two stylized crossed boughs within those sprays is "Mother," particularly appropriate if one accepts a classic definition of a cartouche to be an oval or oblong figure containing a sovereign's name. Additional blocks of tribute, both signed and unsigned and from numerous hands, are set with bright blue sashing to surround the more splendid statement: a jaunty horse and rider (no. 99) and fanciful trees (no. 100) are cut from a red cotton print; a dear little pink rooster beneath a rose and buds already encircled by small green hearts (no. 101) enlivens the unquilted top (no. 102), as do the carefully arranged oak leaves supporting a single acorn, and bright boxed sprays of tiny flowers (no. 103).

It was, of course, more often the mother who made the quilts, first in anticipation and thereafter in celebration, as her children marked their rites of passage. The first (no. 104) she would usually make alone, but thereafter she might share the pleasure. It is often suggested, but less often substantiated,

that upon reaching his twenty-first birthday a young man in nineteenth-century America would be presented with a freedom quilt, worked within an affectionate circle of mothers, grandmothers, sisters, aunts, cousins, and friends. At least one example (no. 105) does in fact exist, significant in its inscription, "Presented to John W Peterson on his Twenty First birth-day May 27 86."

Several of the initials embroidered within the pieced blocks were entered with a simplicity quite appropriate to the common cotton fabrics from which the quilt was constructed. Most (no. 106) were entered with the embroidered flourishes that suggest access to the patterns of elaborate monograms that appeared in great numbers in the women's periodicals of the time. "One of the accomplishments which every lady should learn and try to excel in, is the ability to mark well in Indelible Ink. Clothes of every kind, and particularly handkerchiefs, are constantly in danger of being lost; and there is no security so great against their total loss, as an intelligible mark."[1] In an 1871 fashion illustration from *La Mode illustrée* (no. 107), the young girl is coincidentally holding a book opened to just such a pattern page, perhaps the one being used by the woman on

99. Mother's Quilt Top (detail)

100. Mother's Quilt Top (detail)

101. Mother's Quilt Top (detail)

the left who seems to be at work on a handkerchief or some other small item of personal linen.

The methods by which these patterns could be applied to both personal and household linen could be applied to pieces of quilt blocks as well:

After having wet and thoroughly dried the article . . . iron it very smoothly. Lay it on a flat smooth surface, and place on it a sheet of *Impression Paper*, (sold by the sheet in many colors,) then place over [it] the pattern you wish to copy, and carefully trace over every part with a moderately sharp instrument; the eye of a bodkin is good. After tracing the pattern, remove the paper, and proceed to mark it over with ink. Lay it in the sun for a day or two, and then wash it. The same process of copying is very good for embroidery of any kind, when the patterns are not very large. . . . Marking in fine colored cotton has been

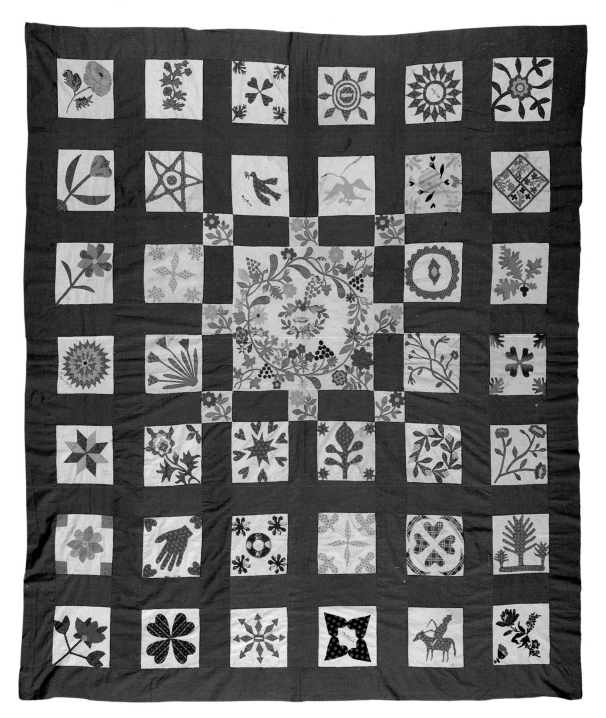

102. Mother's Quilt Top

103. Mother's Quilt Top (detail)

fashionable, and is very pretty. It is done in cross-stitch, or chain-stitch, and requires great neatness to make it ornamental. In selecting cotton for this use, subject it to a thorough boiling to see if the colors will stand.[2]

For John Peterson's mother, the occasion for which those colors were selected and neatly worked may well have been fraught with apprehension, for by the last quarter of the nineteenth century that son would quite likely note his majority by leaving family or farm.

The same women's periodicals that taught her to mark her linen had instructed her on the special importance of raising a son:

> The law of the mother is the guide of the son. The principles she instils into her home-life are never entirely forgotten; she moulds the character of the man. Make your homes pure and perfect, and life will be the same. Every woman has her influence on at least one man, and him she can rule, if she will, for good.[3]

"The law of the mother" found reference in 1855 on the Hoagland quilt (no. 177) with another mother's inscription, "Forsake not the law of thy Mother / Mrs. Hoagland / Prov[erbs] 1st, 8th," and on an album quilt made for William M. Ketcham, upon which a Bible is opened to Psalm XXIII above an inscription, "From Mother 1862. My son, hear the instruction of the Father and forsake not the Law of thy Mother," with slight variation the biblical verse referred to by Mrs. Hoagland.

Even at great distances, the relationship between mothers and daughters remained one of devoted dependency,[4] but a mother may have sensed a fearful finality as a son

104. The Soper Child's Quilt
Inscribed H. O. Soper
United States
Mid-nineteenth century
34 x 29 in. (86.4 x 73.7 cm)
Mr. and Mrs. Thomas H. Morgan

105. The Freedom Quilt
      "Presented to John W Peterson on his
      Twenty First birth-day"
      United States
      1886
      68¾ x 81¾ in. (174.6 x 206.4 cm)
      Los Angeles County Museum of Art, gift of
      the Betty Horton Collection

106. The Freedom Quilt (detail)

107. From *La Mode illustrée* (1871), unpaginated

guilty abandon and corrupt morals are not indigenous to New York, but flourish in only a lesser degree in all of the great cities."[5] This leave-taking was the subject of a number of late-nineteenth-century books, and of Thomas Hovenden's sentimental painting *Breaking Home Ties* (no. 108), and perhaps of the freedom quilt presented to John W. Peterson on his twenty-first birthday.

For some women, the children they loved were the children of others. These were the women of the "Single Sisterhood," the unmarried sisters and daughters of nineteenth-century America, the "old maids" who are described and defined throughout that period in diaries and journals (their own and others),[6] whose lives provided fertile ground for Victorian fiction and whose stature in society is the very specific subject of one of America's most extraordinary social

left for the West, for a bride and a home of his own, or for the unspeakable perils to be found in such a metropolitan city as New York: "The Great Maelstrom of Vice . . . first in vice, first in wealth, and first in the abominations which curse humanity. . . . [although] the giddy voluptuaries who find pleasure in

108. *Breaking Home Ties* (detail)
Thomas Hovenden (American, 1840–95)
1890
52⅛ x 72¼ in (132.4 x 183.5 cm)
Oil on canvas
Philadelphia Museum of Art, given by Ellen Harrison McMichael in memory of C. Emory McMichael

that it is impossible not to admire them.[7]

These would eventually be the homes of the members of the Young Ladies Sewing Society of the First Congregational Church, who organized themselves in December 1859 for the purposes of moral and intellectual development and for "great fun and fine suppers."[8] They determined to present an album bedquilt bearing all their names to each member on the occasion of her marriage. In the charming diary she kept from her tenth year to her thirtieth (1852–72), one of those young ladies, Caroline Cowles Richards, included details of the members quilting together in Canandaigua in fulfillment of that pledge:

109. View of Canandaigua, New York. Frontispiece, Caroline Cowles Richards, *Village Life in America, 1852–1872* (Williamstown, MA: Corner House, 1972)

documents, a quilt worked in Canandaigua, New York (no. 109), in 1871. Frances Trollope, an English traveler whose three-and-a-half-year journey in America had resulted in the 1832 London publication of her distinctly disdainful observations on the *Domestic Manners of the Americans*, had nevertheless found Canandaigua to be

> as pretty a village as ever man contrived to build. Every house is surrounded by an ample garden, and at that flowery season, they were half buried in roses. It is true these houses are of wood, but they are so neatly painted, in such perfect repair, and show so well within their leafy setting,

110. The Old Maid's Quilt
   Made by the Young Ladies Sewing Society
   of the First Congregational Church
   Canandaigua, New York
   1871
   76 x 68 in. (193 x 172.7 cm)
   Los Angeles County Museum of Art, gift of
   Shelly Zegart

111. The Old Maid's Quilt (detail)

I have been up at Laura Chapin's from 10 o'clock in the morning until 10 at night, finishing Jennie Howell's bed quilt, as she is to be married very soon. Almost all of the girls were there. We finished it at 8 p.m. and when we took it off the frames we gave three cheers.[9] (26 March 1862)

One of the members, Susan Daggett, had determined at the age of eighteen that she wished never to marry, but the others had promised she would have a quilt nevertheless. Both vows were kept, and in 1871, at age thirty, Susie received that token of their affection and, perhaps, of their pity (no. 110). The circumstances of its presentation were recorded in a centennial booklet published by the First Congregational Church in June 1899:

It was the custom of the society to present album quilts, and, later, gold thimbles to its members as bridal gifts, and

any member reaching the age of thirty, being still unmarried, was to receive a quilt. There is, however, a record of only one member, Miss Daggett, being brave enough to acknowledge the attainment of such a great age. The quilt was sent to New Haven, where she resided at that time. Each member of the society made a block, containing her autograph, but in all probabililty the central block was the chief cause of the custom being forever abolished. This block, donated by the pastor, Mr. Allen, consisted of a pen-picture of a spinster with her knitting work [she is in fact threading a sewing needle], with her hair done up in a ridiculous little knot. This, by the way, was not intended to be an exact likeness of any member of the society.[10]

112. *The Schoolmistress* by Darley. Undated. Reproduced from the Collections of the Library of Congress

The quilt's central image (no. 111) is indeed stereotypical of a nineteenth-century spinster, that of a dour, pinch-nosed woman with a dress drawn tight over her thin back and shoulders. That "ridiculous little knot" and the filet work of her mitts places her in the earlier, and therefore unfashionable, style of the 1850s. In addition to its inaccuracy (photographs show Susan as an attractive and fashionable young woman[11]), that "pen-picture" seems unnecessarily cruel, and surely unoriginal as well. It was probably copied from a still-unidentified print source, quite possibly one by the artist Darley, whose portrait *The Schoolmistress* (no. 112) bears a number of similarities in costume and comportment.[12]

Many of the inscribed and autographed blocks[13] seem to accentuate the mocking portrait they surround, more harshly perhaps because they came from the hands of friends: "Old maids are embers on the [illegible] from which sparks have fled. (Nettie Palmer)," for example, and ". . . an old Maid / Once a bright and shining light / But now forever dark / Her light burns out unknown, unsung / She dies without a spark. (unsigned)."

The iconography of the yellow leaves surrounding the portrait is confirmed by this inscription on an unsigned block,

> She dwelt among the untrodden ways
> Beside the springs of Dove.
> A maid whom there were none to praise
> And very few to love."
> Your May of life has fallen
> To the sere, the yellow leaf,

by a similar phrase in *Annals of Pioneer Settlers on the Whitewater and its Tributaries*, published four years later in 1875 ("some who are now in the sear and yellow leaf of life")[14] and, perhaps, by the tiny quilted figure dwarfed by the "sere and yellow leaves" on the border (no. 113) that surrounds a pieced

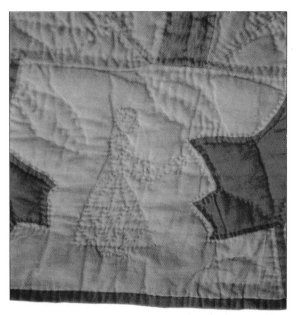

113. Detail of a quilt signed Eliza M. Jackson
United States
Second half nineteenth century
Size unknown

and appliquéd quilt signed Eliza M. Jackson. Emily H. Wheeler had inscribed her contribution to Susan's quilt, "The Melancholy days have come." Perhaps for Eliza Jackson they had come as well.

NOTES

1. Florence Hartley, *The Ladies' Hand Book of Fancy and Ornamental Work* (Philadelphia: J. W. Bradley, 1861), 168.
2. Ibid., 169.
3. *Dorcas Magazine* (December 1884), 307.
4. Carroll Smith-Rosenberg, "The Female World of Love and Ritual: Relations between Women in Nineteenth-Century America," *Signs: Journal of Women in Culture and Society* 1 (1975), no. 1: 15–17.
5. J. W. B., *Metropolitan Life Unveiled: Sunlight and Shadow of America's Great Cities* (Philadelphia: West Philadelphia Publishing, 1891): 25–26.
6. In speaking of his fourteen-year-old cousins, Lucy and Rozelle, young Jesse Applegate

remembered that in the days of his journey to Oregon, "girls from twelve to seventeen were young ladies. Over that age they were called old maids. Old maidenhood was frowned upon." and quoted the prevailing sentiment of the times to be "Old age is honorable but / Old maids are abominable." Jesse Applegate, *Recollections of My Boyhood* (Rosewood, OR: Press of Review Publishing, 1914), 56.

7. Frances Trollope, *Domestic Manners of the Americans* (London: Whittaker, Treacher, 1832), 311. In a period of intense national pride, Americans were particularly sensitive to foreign criticism and Mrs. Trollope's lengthy recitation of observed personal "vulgarities" was, understandably, ill-received in this country.

8. Caroline Cowles Richards, *Village Life in America 1852–1872* (Williamstown, MA: Corner House, 1972), 2.

9. Ibid., 140. In Jacqueline Marx Atkins, *Shared Threads: Quilting Together — Past and Present* (New York: Viking Studio Books, 1994) two illustrated quilts (34 and 35) are attributed to the Young Ladies Sewing Society.

10. *100th Anniversary Booklet of the First Congregational Church, Canandaigua, N.Y.,* June 1899, 64.

11. Susan Daggett was an accomplished young woman. From 1878–80 she served as assistant lady principal at Vassar College, but she found her primary vocation within the church, serving for fourteen years as the president of a woman's board of missions in New Haven. Shelly Zegart, "Old Maid-New Woman," *The Quilt Digest* 4 (1986).

12. I am grateful to Mary Jaene Edmonds for bringing *The Schoolmistress* to my attention.

13. The blocks are transcribed in full in Sandi Fox, *Wrapped in Glory: Figurative Quilts & Bedcovers 1700–1900* (New York: Thames and Hudson/Los Angeles County Museum of Art, 1990), 101–03.

14. *Annals of Pioneer Settlers on the Whitewater and its Tributaries in the Vicinity of Richmond, Ind., from 1804 to 1830* (Richmond, IN: Press of the Telegram Printing Company, 1875), 27.

Gently Rest Beneath These Pieces Joined by Friendly Hands for Thee

The Emmaus Church in New Kent County, Virginia (see dedication page), was dedicated in September 1852, and it was decided thereafter that the ladies of the congregation would present to their pastor a token of their affection and esteem. On the elaborate quilt block (no. 114) she worked as her contribution to the whole (no. 115), Nannie Christian inscribed a faintly familiar verse —

> Friendship's Offering / Whose silent eloquence more rich / than words, tell of the giver's faith / And truth in absence, and says / "Forget Me Not" —

that had been written, with slight variation, on a simple pieced cotton quilt (no. 116) five years earlier:

> This is Affection's Tribute, Friendship's Offering: / Whose silent eloquence, more rich than words, / Tells of the writers faith and truth in absence. / And says — Forget Me-not!

Two phrases appearing in both, "Friendship's Offering" and "Forget Me Not," joined with a third, "Remember Me," as those seemingly written more often than any others in the 1830s on the pages of autograph albums and a decade later on the pages that had become quilt blocks. Within the 169 signed blocks that form the geometrically constructed peaks and valleys of the Delectable Mountains, there are six additional verses requesting remembrance, both simply ("Remember me when this you see") and sentimentally ("Forget me not — but let thy memory linger / As a soft, shadowy twilight, in thy mind: / And like a harp, touched by some fairy finger / my voice shall whisper through the evening mind — Forget me not").

Beyond the sentimental excesses of Victorian verse, and the perhaps prerequisite number of biblical quotations and several memorial verses and moral admonitions, a large number of the inscriptions on that quilt are of a more factual nature. Through them we know, for example, that "This Bedquilt commenced in 1839 / And finished in 1847." Many of the signers are probably Baptist (two ministers of that denomination are noted, one of whom was "Revd Charles J. Hopkins/ [who] Preached his farewell sermon in the / Baptist Ch in Bridgeton Sept 24th 1843 . . . Removed to New York City."

114. The Emmaus Church Quilt (detail)

As was the Reverend Charles Hopkins, several parishioners noted on the blocks were "removed" to Georgia, Kentucky, Massachusetts, New Hampshire, New York, Ohio, and Pennsylvania:

> Elisha S. Barrath / Removed to Ohio / 1839.

> Rosannah J. Swinney / Albany / Georgia / Whose lot is cast in a strange land.

> Daniel S. Swinney / Mansfield Ohio / Far distant from his / native home.

By including them on this quilt, they are present though absent. The balance of locations, where noted, are from New Jersey: Camden,[1] Hopewell, New Germantown, Newark, Plainfield, and Shiloh, for example, and more than thirty are marked Bridgeton, New Jer-

sey, where the quilt was in all probability organized, pieced, and quilted. This quilt is the object of ongoing research, but it was certainly made for, and probably the creation of, Mrs. Ruth B. Ogden of that town. A number of the dedicatory blocks, as they so often were, are addressed in a manner that allows for the connection of kinship: "Respected Aunt," "Dear Aunt," and "To my mother," for example. Although all those signed or honored appear to be family or friends, at least one was not; on 7 August 1844, Eliza P. Grunzebach wrote, "Dear Mrs. Ogden / I have not the pleasure of a / personal acquaintance yet I have taken / the liberty of sending a small token of love." In Bridgeton, on 17 October 1843, midway through the gathering of its blocks, Margarett Satheld [?] wrote on her contribution to Mrs. Ogden's quilt, "How sweet the thoughts of early

115. The Emmaus Church Quilt
      Made for Dr. John G. Carter by the ladies of
      the Emmaus Church
      New Kent County, Virginia
      1852
      101 x 86 in. (256.6 x 218.4 cm)
      Valentine Museum

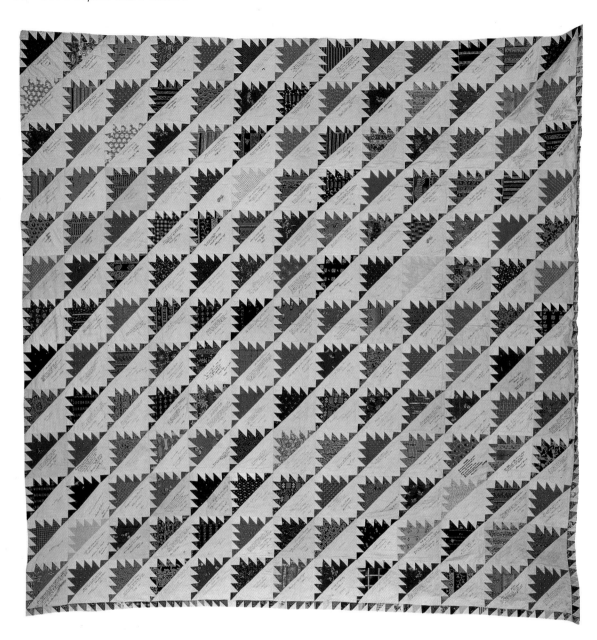

116. Mrs. Ogden's Delectable Mountains Quilt
Made for, and probably by, Mrs. Ruth B.
Ogden
Probably Bridgeton, New Jersey
Marked 1839–47
102 x 100 in. (259.1 x 254 cm)
Abby Aldrich Rockefeller Folk Art Center,
Williamsburg, Virginia

117. The Delectable Mountains Quilt
Probably New Jersey
Marked 1842–43
95 x 94 in. (241.3 x 238.8 cm)
Los Angeles County Museum of Art, American Quilt Research Center Acquisition Fund

118. The Delectable Mountains Quilt (detail)

119. The Delectable Mountains Quilt (detail)

friends and scenes, / All else may fade these linger to the last." In that same year, other friends and other scenes were being entered on another New Jersey quilt (no. 117), its Delectable Mountains worked in an important catalogue of that period's turkey red printed cottons. Several blocks were signed in Burlington, Salem, and Union county locations.

This more formal quilt was worked with greater technical proficiency and presents a more inventive and fully realized border,[2] and it differs substantially in the inscriptive material on its surface. Its 113 pieced blocks are set diagonally in alternating rows, and of these more than thirty bear no discernible signature. Where there are signatures (and occasionally locations), fewer than thirty additionally bear verses. Of those, Mary F. Coward has inscribed "Friendship" and Sarah B. Ballinger has asked "Remember Me," but the others have written almost exclusively brief biblical verses (no. 118) or phrases. If the inscriptions on this quilt are

fewer in number and less diverse and factual in nature than those on Mrs. Ogden's quilt, their imaginative and delicate embellishment provides an extensive and visually poetic illustration of the vocabulary of motifs used on the most elegant of these pieces. A winged angel holds an open book and trails above her flying form a ribbon bearing the name of Ann Eliza Taylor (no. 119), and Elizabeth Ballentyne's signature appears beneath a pensively posed woman, holding fast to an anchor as the sea swirls around the small rock on which she is seated[3] (no. 120). Among the motifs that surround many of the other signatures, or are worked above or below them, are two birds on intertwined boughs holding between their beaks a leafy circle (a motif also used somewhat later on the Quaker silk quilt (see no. 55) bearing multiple New Jersey names); an open book and quill pen in the middle of an open oval wreath; a palette with brushes atop two books; and a pair of kissing cherubs seated on a garland-draped arrow in the middle of

120. The Delectable Mountains Quilt (detail)

121. The Delectable Mountains Quilt (detail)

an illuminated cloud. A tiny penned landscape (no. 121) appears in astounding detail, with thatched-roof cottage, trees and garden, bird and picket fence, and a bridge crossing a small stream in which anglers drift in a rowboat. Beneath this pastoral scene: ". . Around thy habitation . . . . / . May peace scatter roses . . . . /. And the canopy of content . . / Shield thy hours from sorrow. / . Mrs. Harriet Stevens. / .May 18th 1843."

By the last quarter of the nineteenth century, the realistically developed images that characterized so many of those early friendship quilts, either as appliquéd album blocks or as small penned pictures, are seen less often on America's cotton quilts. The signatures are now more often simply written or embroidered in cotton floss, increasingly on geometric pieced blocks, either singly or gathered together as on an 1880s sampler quilt (nos. 122 and 123) found in Canton, Ohio. The principal theme on this Ohio quilt would seem to be its pieced and quilted flags (those of Egypt and Germany among those

joining the Stars and Stripes), but two other blocks are of particular interest. The tombs — so realistically rendered in the mourning arts of the early nineteenth century — appear in simple, stylized shapes on this quilt: beneath "A Stranger A Friend" (left block, no. 124), three crosses stand on a plinth inscribed "I Have Suffered," and an 1888 date appears on a multitiered construction (center block, no. 125) identified at least by the late 1890s, in periodicals and in such mail-order pattern catalogues as those from Ladies Art Company, as Garfield's Monument. Republican President James A. Garfield, an Ohio native, was shot in the Washington railway station on 2 July 1881, and succumbed to blood poisoning caused by his wounds on 19 September 1881. His presidency was short and ineffectual, but the dramatic circumstances of his death caused him also to be the subject of an extensive number of printed silk memorial ribbons that eventually worked their way onto the surfaces of that period's silk and velvet crazy quilts.

122. The Foreign Flags Quilt
Possibly Canton, Ohio
Marked 1888
83⅜ x 72⅝ in. (211.8 x 184.5 cm)
Laura Fisher/Antique Quilts & Americana, NYC

It is often difficult to determine the true extent of group participation on a friendship quilt, to identify the divisions of labor in the making and the gathering of blocks and/or signatures, and in the final quilting itself. This is certainly true in the case of the flag-filled Ohio quilt, and of another sampler quilt (nos. 126 and 127) composed of forty-nine blocks, quilted diagonally, and possibly of Pennsylvania origin. Two sets of initials and one signature are embroidered on three of those blocks, but on each of the others the signature is only written in pencil on a slip of paper affixed tenuously to the block's colorful surface. Were these the names of the makers of each individual block, pleased to

123. The Foreign Flags Quilt

124. The Foreign Flags Quilt (detail)

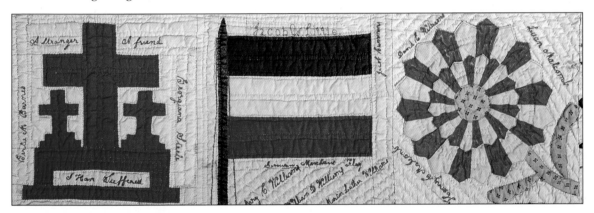

125. The Foreign Flags Quilt (detail)

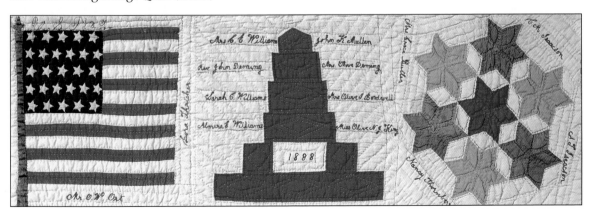

126. The Sampler Friendship Quilt
      Possibly Pennsylvania
      Circa 1880
      75¾ x 75¾ in. (192.4 x 192.4 cm)
      Los Angeles County Museum of Art, gift of
      "To a Friend's House" Project

127. The Sampler Friendship Quilt (detail)

be asked to cut and piece but reluctant technically or time-wise to embroider their names or initials? Did the quiltmaker responsible for the quilt's final assembly also assume the task of transferring names to blocks, and then tire after the completion of the first three? Several stacks of quilt blocks in private collections do bear similar paper identification on each block, but they had yet to be sewn together into the quilt's top. This piece has already been quilted, after which it would have been much more difficult to add an embroidered identification. Here the slips of paper differ and are both lined and unlined; a variety of writing instruments were used, but the entries are primarily in pencil; and they are generally individually written signatures. They each bear one other perplexing notation in the form of a two-digit number; they are not drawn from a consecutive series, and because of the range in which they fall seem most probably to be the age of each individual. The quilt was never washed or used, and with the exception of one, carefully saved, the slips of paper remain affixed.

The most modest participation in the making of a friendship quilt required nothing more than taking pen in hand to enter one's name on a block prepared by another, but that small act was eagerly sought and gratefully accepted and has always been considered an integral part of quilting together in America. Those blocks were most often identical in pattern, as were thirty-two Carolina Lilys, brightly sashed and bordered (no. 128). The embroidered edges seen on Nannie Christian's padded and layered blossoms (see no. 114) were replaced with the clean sharp lines of that classic pieced and appliquéd pattern, and Nannie's embellished leaves and twisting tendrils appear on this work in stylized form, quilted in tiny, white running stitches on a border then completed with a row of Sawteeth constructed from the large number of red cotton prints from which the geometric petals were cut (no. 129). These vigorous repetitive patterns came to define for many the distinctly American quilt.

128. The Carolina Lily Quilt
      Probably Pennsylvania
      Third quarter nineteenth century
      89 x 103 in. (226.1 x 261.6 cm)
      Dr. Byron and Sara Dillow

129. The Carolina Lily Quilt (detail)

NOTES

1. At least sixteen of the Pennsylvania blocks are from Philadelphia, just across the Delaware River from Camden, New Jersey.
2. The simple Sawtooth border on Mrs. Ogden's quilt, perfectly appropriate for its less formal central panel, is inexplicably missing from the top and from the quilt's left side.
3. One of the printed sources for motifs similar to this was women's periodicals of the period, but the author has long suspected, but cannot confirm, that some of these statue-like figures were copied from those engravings of actual statues frequently illustrated in published local and state histories. *The Statistics and Gazetteer of New-Hampshire*, Alonzo J. Fogg (Concord, NH: D. L. Guernsey, 1874), opp. p. 588), contains an engraved illustration of a twenty-four-foot solid granite monument then standing on Dustin's Island, near the mouth of the Contoocook. It was dedicated to the memory of Mrs. Hannah Dustin, and her seven-foot statue atop the monument is stylistically similar to the sketch of our rock-bound lady, although Mrs. Dustin stands, defiant, holding the axe with which she is said to have delivered the death-blow to ten of her Indian captors!

130. The Boston Street Aid Society Quilt
Made to commemorate the history of the
Boston Street Aid Society, 1851–86
Lynn, Essex County, Massachusetts
1886
87 x 87 in. (221 x 221 cm)

Woman's Work Is Never Done

The spire on the Boston Street Methodist Church is seen through the trees in the center of an 1864 sketch (no. 131) of Lynn, Massachusetts, just as Lynn itself stood as the center of Methodism in Massachusetts.[1] It was in this tranquil setting that the ladies of the Boston Street Aid Society had labored for more than a dozen years. In 1886, that society's beginnings and the results of those labors were entered in ink on a red and white pieced quilt (no. 130) that now also serves to define and confirm those areas in which ladies aid societies across America consistently contributed to both church and community.

Certainly the members looked forward with pleasure to the cordial company of their peers, but the reference on the quilt to the first meeting of the Boston Street Aid Society (no. 132) clearly indicates that when the original twenty-seven members first met on 21 May 1851, they met for purpose: "[They] assessed themselves One dollar and fifty cents a year, and agreed to bind <u>Shoes</u> to add money to the Treasury for the purpose of furnishing the interior of the M.E. Church to be erected on Park Street. or Boston Street."

The founders of the society were a small band of devoted Christian Women . . . .The [monthly] meetings were held at their residences. At the hour named for meeting, might be seen the two managers trudging along with their huge carpet-bags filled with shoes for the afternoon's work. At 3 and 5 o'clock the Secretary called the roll and all not answering to their names were fined 6¼ cents per call, while those present were at work binding shoes. [Members who worked on shoes were credited 12½ cents per meeting toward their yearly assess- ment.[2]] They bound from 36 to 128 pairs at each meeting. At sun-down they were invited to tea, which by a fixed rule, consisted of milk-biscuit, cheese, one kind of cake, and tea. This rule was strictly adhered to.[3]

In fact, shoes had long been an important part of Lynn's economy. In February 1800, the legislature passed an act to encourage the manufacture of shoes, boots, and "goloshes,"[4] and by 1810 women were a considerable part of the labor pool: "It appeared, by careful

131. "View in Lynn." Frontispiece from Alonzo Lewis and James R. Newhall, *History of Lynn, Essex County, Massachusetts* (Boston: John L. Shorey, 1865)

estimation, that there were made in Lynn, this year, 1,000,000 pairs of shoes, valued at about $800,000. The females earned some $50,000 by binding."[5] For those ladies who decided to undertake this avenue of potential charitable income, it seems to have been a logical and profitable choice.

The church (no. 133) was indeed built on Boston and New Park streets.[6] It was dedicated on 9 June 1853, and several "Summary" entries on the quilt's surface suggest that for the thirty-five years recorded on that historical textile the society assumed responsibility for much of the church's embellishment and maintenance. In addition to those contributions one might perhaps expect of a nineteenth-century "ladies society" (settees and curtains for a parlor, crockery for the kitchen, chairs and carpet for the altar in the vestry, for example), the society also undertook the purchase of gas pipes for the church[7] and a furnace for the parsonage, and assumed the church's $600 floating debt.

132. The Boston Street Aid Society Quilt (detail) "At / Lynn / Massachusetts / May 21.1851. / Twenty seven persons / met at the residence of / James Pool Jr. / and at the first meeting of the / Boston Street Aid Society /assessed themselves One dollar and fifty / cents a year, and agreed to bind Shoes to add / money to the Treasury for the purpose of fur- / nishing the interior of the M.E./ Church to be erected on Park Street. or Boston Street."

133. Stereograph (detail)
     Undated view of the Boston Street
     Methodist Church
     Lynn Historical Society

134. The Boston Street Aid Society Quilt (detail)
     "Summary / 1871. / An appeal from the /
     Western States that were / devastated by fire
     was rec. / and the Soc responded by /
     bringing their sewing machines to the
     Church vestry and ma- / nufacturing gar-
     ments, bedding etc. / The vestry was
     opened for one / week and the result was
     eight / hundred garments, bedding etc.
     valu-/ ed at $400.00 which were sent to Mi-
     / chigan and rec. by Relief comee and /
     acknowledged by Gov. Baldwin."

Adhering to tradition, the society supported its missions abroad ("Also sent to Mrs. Dr. Butler of India one large box of useful and fancy articles, suitable for a fair.") and provided assistance to individual parishioners at home. The quilt notes the contribution of $65 to Sisters Goodwin and Tarbox, who had been burned out of their homes. Devastating fires were an ever-present occurrence in Lynn: during the year (1864) in which John Andrew Sheldon sketched that idyllic view looking down from Forest Place (see no. 131), for example, Benjamin Reed's "fine summer residence" was destroyed, as was the schoolhouse on Howard Street, George Emery's soap manufacturing establishment, Isaac Tarbox's bakery (along with his frame house), and (barely two months after the arrival of the city's first steam fire engine), city hall itself.[8] Neither flames nor the society's compassion were confined to Lynn, and another of the quilt's "Summary" entries (no. 134), this for 1871, records the receipt of "an appeal from the Western States that were devastated by fire" to which the society responded by "bringing their sewing machines to the church vestry and manufactured garments, bedding etc. The vestry was opened for one week and the result was eight hundred garments, bedding etc. valued at $400.00 which were sent to Michigan."

135. "Six and Eighty-Six Knitting for the Soldiers," from Frank B. Goodrich, *The Tribute Book: A Record of the Munificence, Self-Sacrifice and Patriotism of the American People During the War for the Union* (New York: Derby & Miller, 1865)

But the most significant entries on the Boston Street Aid Society quilt are those detailing the society's response to the national conflagration that was the Civil War.

By the middle of May 1861, armed with needles and thread, small groups of women across the country had set themselves to the task of providing for an entire army that which they had always provided for their families (no. 135). To the sewing of shirts, the knitting of socks, the making of bedding, and the preparation of cordials and preserves, they added the scraping of lint and the rolling of bandages. Their industry was generally frustrated, however, by their ignorance of the numbers needed and methods of distribution until the newly formed Women's Central Association of Relief brought an orderly direction to their patriotic determination. This organization was, in turn, absorbed

into the newly formed United States Sanitary Commission, a philanthropic commission of extraordinary magnitude and complexity.[9] Auxiliary societies and branches of that commission were soon established, with the New England Women's Auxiliary Association being organized in Boston on 12 December 1861. But the Boston Street Aid Society had not been idle.

On April 16, four days after the attack of Fort Sumter, two full companies of armed militia, the Lynn Light Infantry and the Lynn City Guards, had gone to war. The quilt records that the society issued the first call for "a public meeting at Lyceum Hall of all the citizens who were willing to contribute toward aiding the Sanitary Commission in sending stores to aid the sick and wounded Soldiers. The result was a large gathering forming themselves into Ward Com.ees to work for the object. The trustees loaned the use of the Church vestry and several large boxes were sent."

Letters of acknowledgment from the Sanitary Commission were copied onto the quilt and each is dated (October 28, November 5, November 11, and November 21) prior to the organization of the New England Women's Auxiliary Association.[10] The fifth transcribed letter of acknowledgement (undated) is in fact from the auxiliary's headquarters on Summer Street in Boston where women and men met daily to unpack, sort, repack, and forward the donations:

> I have the pleasure to acknowledge the rec. of a most welcome box of supplies from the B. St. Aid Soc. of Lynn. The box shall be sent today on its way to our Army before Richmond to give its share of aid and comfort to those who stand so sorely in need.

Women knew, earlier by instinct and now by instruction, what their soldiers

136. The Boston Street Aid Society Quilt (detail) "List of contents / of boxes sent to / the Sanitary Com- /mission 1861. / Comforters 32. Pillows 23 / Sheets 22. Pillow cases 23 / Large roll of old Pillow cases. Sheets /etc. Large bundles of old linnens lint./ Flannel Shirts 19. Bleached Shirts 10. / Flannel drawers 19. 3 Dressing gowns. / large bundle Hand'k's. 3 Blankets. 6 prs. / slippers. Towels, napkins, woolen shawls, / Bandages, Pin Balls, Quilts, cushions. / Large lot of station-ary. medicines. Cor- / dials. preserves etc. etc. in large quantities. / all of which were duly acknowledged / by the Officers of the U. S. Sanitary / Commission."

gowns. / large bundle Hand'k's. 3 Blankets, 6 prs / slippers. Towels, napkins, woolen shawls, / Bandages, Pin balls, Quilts, cush-ions. / large lot of stationery, medicines, cor- / dials, preserves etc. etc. in large quanti-ties." The first great wave of donations was drawn from closets and shelves and trunks, and when it became necessary to resort to those items made new, such fundraising activities as the large sanitary fairs raised money to buy materials. Personal messages accompanied the early donations, both old and new: "My son is in the army. Whoever is made warm by this quilt, which I have worked on for six days and almost all of six nights, let him remember his own mother's love."; "This blanket was carried by Millie Aldrich, who is ninety-three years old, down hill and up hill, one and a half miles, to be given to some soldier."; "This pillow belonged to my little boy, who died resting on it; it is a precious treasure to me, but I give it for the soldiers."[11] But those were written in the early years of the war, and when the shelves were bare and the trunks were empty, the time for sentiment more often yielded to the demands of a frenzied pace of production. Even historic linens had been given over to the cause: the New Haven Soci-ety received a sheet bearing cross-stitched initials ("J.*.E.") more than 100 years old, and in 1862 in Lancaster, Pennsylvania, Mrs. Mary Witmer scraped into lint the linen she had woven in 1812 from flax she had spun.[12] When these too were gone it fell, for exam-ple, to the Albany Relief Society to include in its ninety-seven boxes of hospital stores and clothing the one thousand pillowcases made by Miss Skerritt's pupils, and the four hun-dred and forty sheets made by the young ladies of the Female Academy.[13]

Each of the letters of acknowledgement, both from the Sanitary Commission and later from the Michigan Relief Society, are addressed to Miss Abby M. Newhall. Miss

would need. The "List of contents of boxes sent to the Sanitary Commission 1861" (no. 136) could have been one drawn from any number of contributing individuals and organizations: "Comforters 32. Pillows 23 / Sheets 22 / Pillow cases 23 / Large roll of old Pillow cases, Sheets / etc. Large bundles of old linnen lint, / Flannel Shirts 19. Bleached Shirts 10. / Flannel drawers 19. 3 Dressing

137. The Bear Lake Stake Quilt
     Quilted inscription: Made by the St. Charles
     Relief Society September 14th 1881
     St. Charles, Idaho
     90½ x 77 in. (229.9 x 195.6 cm)
     International Society Daughters of Utah
     Pioneers
     Pioneer Memorial Museum

138. *A Quilting Bee in the Olden Time*
H. W. Peirce
Delaware
Circa 1876
Courtesy of the Society for the Preservation
of New England Antiquities

Newhall's name was closely associated with the Boston Street Methodist Church (and indeed with Lynn itself, as a descendant of Thomas Newhall, the first white child born in the settlement, in 1630) having served the Boston Street Aid Society in an official position for forty-eight consecutive years, including more than twenty-four years as secretary (1855–80) and twenty-one years as president.[14] Hers is the name entered most often and most prominently throughout the quilt, suggesting the probability that she was in some way involved with the making of the quilt, or certainly the possibility that the quilt was at some point given as a tribute to the woman who had been so instrumental in the activities it was inscribed to celebrate.

In its recording of a church-related history on the surface of a quilt, with the participation of (or possibly presentation to) a venerable leader, this Methodist quilt is, in concept, not unlike those worked by other religious denominations throughout the

nineteenth century and into the next. An Idaho quilt (no. 137), for example, sets down the organization of the Bear Lake Stake of the Church of Jesus Christ of Latter-day Saints in 1877. Mormons place a particular emphasis on the recording of church history, so it is not unexpected to find the inclusion of extensively detailed information on the large number of wards the stake encompassed. Where the Boston quilt is inscribed with notations as to the establishing dates of its Sunday school and the ladies aid society, the Bear Lake quilt records its Mormon counterparts, the primary association, and the women's relief society. But if concept and content bear certain similarities, the elaborately embroidered central motif and spandrels of the Idaho quilt are in sharp contrast to the crisp abstraction of the sturdy Massachusetts quilt, and the western quilt (backed with a delicate blue cashmere) is finely and imaginatively quilted with multiple floral patterns. A quilted inscription has been worked above its lower border, "Made by St. Charles Relief Society September 14th 1881," and it was later presented to Annie Bryson Laker,[15] whose name appears in the lower right-hand corner as president of the primary association. It was a position she held for more than twenty years.[16]

139. The Boston Street Aid Society Quilt (detail)
      "1851 Boston St. Aid Society. 1886."
      "... 1886 / Abby M. Newhall, Pres ...."

With the demands of the war and the western fires behind them, the Boston Street Aid Society quilt records that in 1876 the members

> Held a centennial meeting at which the members and friends dressed in "ancient" costume, and relics of the past century were exhibited, much to the entertainment and instruction of all present. A bountifull supper of "ye olden dishes" was served by waiters in "ye olden time" and a handsome sum of money realized for our soc. treasury.[17]

Similar events were a staple of the centennial celebrations, leading to their illustration in a number of such popular prints as *A Quilting Bee in the Olden Time* (no. 138). Although the peacock feathers in the corner are among its several interior inconsistencies,

the ladies gathered around the frame dressed in "ancient costume" (calash, quilted petticoat, reticules, etc.) are presented in a reasonably accurate picture of quilting together in America. The quilt in the frame seems to be designed as a pieced top in the English center medallion tradition; in the lower-right corner, small pieced blocks tumble from a basket bearing the artist's initials, HWP; the woman standing top right is measuring the quilt's border; the woman at the lower left of the frame is probably marking the piece for quilting with a chalk-dusted string; behind her, an older quiltmaker has moved closer to the light from the window in order to thread her needle.

Abby M. Newhall and the Boston Street Aid Society had once again turned their attention to their original mission. The quilt records that between 1880 and 1886, the society repaired the church vestibule; papered the parsonage; purchased knives, forks, and spoons for the use of church meetings; paid the balance on the parsonage debt; refitted the church with water pipes; remodeled the kitchen; and then gave to the Trustees of Boston St. M. E. Church $500, the first gift toward a new parsonage. Woman's work is never done! (no. 139)

NOTES

1. The first Methodist society in the state was organized in Lynn, and it was the site of the first Methodist church in Massachusetts. The first Methodist Sunday school in New England met in Lynn, and the first Methodist missionary society in the United States was organized there in 1819. William Henry Meredith, ed., *An Account of the Fifty-First Anniversary of the Boston Street Methodist Episcopal Church, and of Methodist Beginnings in Lynn, Massachusetts* (Published for the church, 1904), 15–16.
2. *An Account of the Commemoration of the Twenty-Fifth Anniversary of the Boston Street M.E. Church, Lynn, Mass., May 20, 1878* (Lynn, MA: n.p., 1880), 28.

3. Meredith, *An Account*, 72.

4. Alonzo Lewis and James R. Newhall, *History of Lynn, Essex County, Massachusetts* (Boston: John L. Shorey, 1865), 361.

5. Ibid., 371.

6. Laurel Nilsen, curator, Lynn Historical Society & Museum, identifies this image (see no. 133) as the earliest known view of the Boston Street Methodist Church. Ms. Nilsen provided copies of a number of those period publications held in their library that pertain to the early history of the Boston Street Methodist Church, and the author acknowledges her important research assistance.

7. In the spring of 1854, the deaths of a number of grand and ancient elms throughout Lynn were locally ascribed to the effects of gas that had leaked from the town's underground pipes. Lewis, *History of Lynn*, 439.

8. Lewis, *History of Lynn*, 477–78.

9. Frank B. Goodrich, *The Tribute Book: A Record of the Munificence, Self-Sacrifice and Patriotism of the American People During the War for the Union* (New York: Derby & Miller, 1865), chapters III and IV. For additional reading on the Sanitary Commission, the author recommends two articles by Virginia Gunn: "Western Reserve Women and the U.S. Sanitary Commission, 1861–1865" in *Western Reserve Studies*, Vol. 3, 1988, pp. 75–85 and "Quilts for Union Soldiers in the Civil War" in *Quiltmaking in America: Beyond the Myths* (Nashville: Rutledge Hill, 1994), 80–95.

10. The Sanitary Aid Society of Lynn was not organized until January 1863. At its 1865 annual meeting they reviewed their activities in 1864, and noting that for eleven weeks their attention had been diverted to working on the sailors' fair, they urged that production efforts now be redoubled: "Surely, in these days of sewing machines, when it takes so short a time to make a shirt, a pair of sheets, or a dressing gown, there are not many in our midst who are not willing to give of their leisure, or even some portion of their busy hours, and thus, by making one of these articles once a month, or oftener, contribute to the comfort of those who are now giving how much more for us." Unidentified newspaper. Lynn, Massachusetts, January 1865.

11. Goodrich, *Tribute*, 153.

12. Goodrich, *Tribute*, 155.

13. Goodrich, *Tribute*, 129.

14. Meredith, *An Account*, 73.

15. Object file, International Society Daughters of Utah Pioneers, Pioneer Memorial Museum.

16. *Deseret Evening News* (9 February 1900): 11.

17. During the Civil War, the Brooklyn and Long Island Sanitary Fair employed a similar device in its reconstruction of a "New England Kitchen," a quilting party being one of the elements included in their attempt to reproduce "the manners, customs, dress, and, if possible, the idiom of the time; in short to illustrate the domestic life and habits . . . .just prior to the throwing overboard of the tea in Boston Harbor." Goodrich, *Tribute*, 195–98.

140. The "God Loveth a Cheerful Giver" Quilt
(detail)
United States
Late nineteenth century
68¾ x 83 in. (174.6 x 210.8 cm)
Private Collection

For God Loveth a Cheerful Giver

There is a certain delicate formality about those names entered on "Mifs Coffin"s Newbury blocks. "Elizabeth" had signed with only her given name, but the fact that all others had signed with full names did not negate the intimacy of their relationships to Hannah Coffin. In a period in which mothers, daughters, sisters, aunts, and cousins often bore the same name, perhaps only detailed attribution could firmly identify such pieces, and the tender sentiments inscribed thereon were the acceptable familiarities of a treasured circle of family and friends. But those circles widened, and women increasingly entered new spheres of interest and expectations. By the 1860s, her church and community and the great social causes of the nineteenth century were increasingly the recipients of a quiltmaker's efforts. The quiltmaker had found within her sewing basket the tools for fundraising, and she used them to great advantage.

Where the request had once been for elaborate blocks, gathered and given as individual affirmations of friendship, now the request was often for simple signatures and small sums, the signatures for the quilt tops, the coins for the coffers. In addition to whatever altruistic motives may be properly assigned to those who gathered and those who gave, the popularity of fundraising quilts must also be considered in light of the great popularity of the autograph itself. In 1889, a Michigan contributor to *Good Housekeeping* magazine observed: "This is a day of autograph hunters. The epidemic assumes various forms. Some have the craze for postal albums. One lady of my acquaintance has an album of several hundred postals from people she admits she never saw and never expects to see."[1] Likewise, fundraising quilts did not require familiarity, only names and numbers: for a Methodist church in Linden, Iowa, "Names cost 10¢ to be embroidered by the women and Allie Lisle twisted most of the arms in town."[2]

The spokes of wheel-type patterns, and/or the spaces between them, proved to be a particularly practical and popular area on which to enter or to acknowledge individual donations. In appliquéd blue and white cotton, thirty Wheel(s) of Fortune rolled across an unidentified community gathering donations for the Mt. Zion Church (no. 141), and the shared space between each spoke (no. 142) yielded fifty cents: "Sylvester Reed / 25 cts/ W.H. Kiel 25 ct," and "Hannah Laughlin / 50 c / Jennie Corbett," for example.

141. The Mt. Zion Quilt
      Possibly Ohio
      1898
      83¾ x 73¾ in. (212.5 x 187.3 cm)
      Los Angeles County Museum of Art, Ameri-
      can Quilt Research Center Acquisition
      Fund, purchased with funds provided by
      the Southern California Council of Quilt
      Guilds

142. The Mt. Zion Quilt (detail)

143. The Mt. Zion Quilt (detail)

Elsewhere (no. 143), an inked inscription identifies the quilt as a "Memento / Of / Ladies Aid Society / Mt. Zion," notes the officers of the Society, records "Rev. C. F. Floto. / Pastor. / Mt. Zion," and the date "Sept 30 1898." The connection between faith and funding was emphasized on another quilt, embroidered on the outer ring of one of its turkey red wheels: II Cor. IX. 7, "For God Loveth a Cheerful Giver" (no. 140).

By that closing decade of the nineteenth century, embroidered outline quilts, most often in a turkey red thread on a white ground, were enjoying great popularity. Pre-stamped "penny blocks" or kits were available in a variety of thematic patterns, but it was a series of original blocks that were worked in 1891 by the Ladies Aid Society of the Methodist Church of Dayton, Indiana, for its annual Harvest Bazaar quilt[3] (no. 144). Many of the blocks are embroidered with geometric patterns that might have been worked on other quilts in plain and printed cottons, particularly inventive in the devel-

opment of circular designs in concentric and overlapping circles. Of special interest, however, are those blocks that identified the currently popular concept of pictorial designs worked in red thread, and in the motifs the quiltmakers chose to render in simple red lines we can see they have drawn from the same vocabulary of designs that characterized earlier and more complex quilts, such as: the single floral motifs (blocks 1D, 6C, and 6F) and both closed and open wreaths (blocks 6D and 6E) earlier cut or constructed from chintz and applied to the Boardman quilt (see no. 40), and the serpent (block 3A)[4] seen with the dove on the red and green bedcover (see no. 89). Flanked by the images of angels, the central field on the Indiana quilt is dominated by the Holy Bible (no. 145), worked within crossed boughs of leaves and berries, and acorns and oak leaves. The opened book's left page is marked 2 Cor. VIII.C.7.v. but as on the red wheel (see no. 140), its very appropriate text is actually from the seventh verse of chapter 9: "Every man

144. The Ladies Aid Society Quilt
      Made by the Ladies Aid Society of the
      Dayton Methodist Church
      Dayton, Tippecanoe County, Indiana
      1891
      84 x 84 in. (213.4 x 213.4 cm)
      Tippecanoe County Historical Association,
      Lafayette, Indiana, donated in memory of
      Mable Kemper by Lloyd Kemper, Dorothy
      Kemper Seal, and Lillian Kemper Reppy
      Courtesy of Marguerite Wiebusch

145. The Ladies Aid Society Quilt (detail)

givers" were enthusiastically recorded for the sum of five cents each.

The elaborate pictorial designs on the Indiana quilt would have been a delightful exception to the geometric patterns that more often formed the ledger pages of these ambitious undertakings. Considering the large number still extant, one might reasonably suspect that the typical fundraising quilt of that period and for that purpose was in colorfast turkey red and white, bearing large numbers of signatures, and made within the circle of ladies aid societies, most often Methodist. But in smaller numbers, both concept and color were also used to raise funds in support of the great social causes of the nineteenth century.[5]

Beyond their usual domestic duties and their religious obligations, many quiltmakers participated fully in the intellectual and social concerns of their community. This was certainly true of Nancy Ellen Boardman in Putnamville, Massachusetts, in 1854–55. In addition to the regular evening meetings with her sewing circle, she attended a variety

according as he purposeth in his heart, so let him give; not grudgingly, or of necessity: for God loveth a cheerful giver." The names of almost nine hundred of those "cheerful

146. The W.C.T.U. Quilt (detail)

147. The W.C.T.U. Quilt
      Union Springs, probably New York
      1896
      76⅞ x 75¼ in. (195.3 x 191.1 cm)
      Los Angeles County Museum of Art, gift of
      the Betty Horton Collection

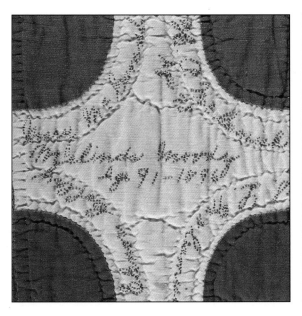

148. The W.C.T.U. Quilt (detail)

149. The Ladies Aid Society Quilt (detail)

of lyceum lectures, including Lucy Stone on "Woman's Rights" and Frederick Douglass on "Slavery," and a series of events on the subject of temperance, including "two excellent sermons from Mr. Fletcher, text p.m. 'Wine is a mocker strong drink is raging.'"[6] Of the three, it was most often in the cause of temperance that the quiltmaker threaded her needle. In Union Springs, New York, more than four decades later, the tradition of fundraising quilts and turkey red was still in evidence with the appropriately patterned Drunkard's Path quilt (no. 146) made to benefit the Woman's Christian Temperance Union (no. 147). Among the donors' names, carefully worked in small red running stitches, is that of "Melinda Moody / Age 91 — 1896" (no. 148). It was a courtesy afforded longevity, as was the recognition of a community's beginnings seen also in the ladies aid society block recording those early settlers of Dayton, Indiana (no. 149).

NOTES

1. Mrs. F.A.W., "Autograph Quilts," *Good Housekeeping,* 26 October 1889, 311.
2. Undated quotation in Dorothy Cozart, "A Century of Fundraising Quilts: 1860–1960," *Uncoverings* 5 (1984): 44.
3. "It was a custom to make these named quilts for sale at the annual Harvest Bazaar." Mrs. Della Dunwoody (one of the oldest living church members), letter, 1979. Quoted in The Indiana Quilt Registry Project, *Quilts of Indiana: Crossroads of Memories* (Bloomington: Indiana University, 1991), 82.
4. Inscribed "And as Moses lifted up / the Serpent in the / wilderness, even so / must the son of man / be lifted up."
5. See Chapter 11, "Other Spheres," in Sandi Fox, *Small Endearments: Nineteenth-Century Quilts for Children and Dolls,* second edition (Nashville: Rutledge Hill, 1994), for additional information and illustration of children's quilts worked in support of the antislavery and temperance movements.
6. *Diaries of Nancy Ellen Boardman,* printed in *Historical Collections of the Danvers Historical Society* 29 (1941): 63.

150. The Snyder Memorial Bedcover
Made by Emily Snyder
Pennsylvania
Mid-nineteenth century
98½ x 98½ in. (250.2 x 250.2 cm)
Los Angeles County Museum of Art, Ameri-
can Quilt Research Center Acquisition Fund

And Departed This Life

Writing of their grandmother's death on the Overland Trail in July 1846, it was important for Virginia Reed to assure her "Dear Couzin" that

> We buried her verry decent We made a nete coffin and buried her under a tree we had made a head stone and had her name cutonit, and the date and yere verry nice, and at the head of the grave was a tree we cut some letters on it.[1]

If their fathers, brothers, and husbands were more often the official keepers of America's public records, women paid particular attention to the safekeeping of its vital statistics. Occasionally this was done in the larger arena (as in the minute-books of the Columbia Maternal Association, the first such statistics in Oregon[2]), but more often the cycles of those lives around them were carefully noted in Bibles, letters, and diaries, and occasionally on their samplers[3] and quilts.

Widowed at the age of twenty-four when her husband was lost at sea, Ann Taylor (Spotsylvania County, Virginia) began to set down a genealogy in small cross-stitches. The inscriptions are marked by their factual simplicity: the date of her birth and that of her husband John; their marriage; the names of their children (William, John, and Ann), young John's death shortly after his second birthday, and finally the death of her husband. She notes that "This was made by Ann Taylor in the year 1798." Modestly embellished with embroidered floral sprays in multicolor silk thread, this piece formed the central segment of her pieced and appliquéd bedcover, which was never finished.[4]

It was perhaps Emily Snyder's widowhood, a half-century later, that impelled her also to work a family register. As did Ann Taylor's work, Emily's record includes the names and dates pertinent to her undertaking, but the manner in which they are recorded, the vigorous images that surround them, and the bright signature blocks that surround the completed panel to form the Snyder memorial bedcover (no. 150) confirm that the European influence on the style of American quilts had waned. In several aspects, Emily's work invites comparison to the family records worked by other Pennsylvania artisans, those *frakturs* worked on paper with watercolor images and inked inscriptions: the familial documentation; the use of calligraphy; religious references; the

151. The Snyder Memorial Bedcover (detail)

traditional folk motifs of tulips and stars; and the color palette in which they are worked.

The cross-stitches employed by Ann Taylor were those traditionally used to mark linens in those closing years of the eighteenth century, but the recording of Emily's joys and sorrows (no. 151) are entered in the newly favored indelible ink:

> Benjamin Snyder, was born, February 22nd / 1794 — and departed this life the 24 / day of October, 1845, Aged 51 years / 8 Months and 2 days.

> Elizabeth Snyder, was born December / 14th 1827 — and departed this life / May 16th 1829 . . Aged 17 months / and 1 day.

> Delia Gordon Snyder, was born / November 17th 1837 and departed / this life September 27th 1838 / Aged 10 months and 12 days

Amanda Snyder, was born April 17th 1826 / and departed this life February 2nd / 1827, aged 8 months and 15 days.

Beneath these griefs are small inked sketches of floral sprays and crossed boughs of leaves, and they are flanked by the names and birth dates of Emily's six surviving children (Lafayette, August 31, 1824; Maria, May 21, 1830; Christopher, September 25, 1832; Benjamin, December 15, 1834; George, September 29, 1839; and Howard, April 12, 1842).[5] Emily entered her own name and date of birth (March 2, 1804) and, among the four verses[6] encircling the central motif, a meaningful admonition:

> How many of us, are another year?
> May sleep beneath the cold & silent sod?
> Then while our lives, are in mercy lengthed here,
> Let us in time prepare to meet our God.

Another family record (no. 152) was never incorporated into a fully realized quilt. Names are entered in the spandrels, held aloft by feathered boughs, and they burst out from the written acknowledgement of their common source: "Father. / Ebenezer Rollins. / Was born / in Deerfield, N.H. / March 22 1781. / He Married Betsey Rollins. / In 180[?] / Moved to Grafton. / N.H." But unlike Emily's entries, or Ann's, the Rollins family register speaks only of life. If Rollins children died young (and in the middle of the nineteenth century they surely did), it is not mentioned. This is the record of the children who survived, and who married, and of those children's children.

NOTES

1. Quoted in Kenneth L. Holmes, ed., *Covered Wagon Women*, Vol. 1, (Glendale, CA: Arthur H. Clark, 1983), 72–73.

152. The Rollins Family Record Quilt Block
United States, probably New Hampshire
Circa 1840
16⅞ x 16¾ in. (42.9 x 42.6 cm)
Abby Aldrich Rockefeller Folk Art Center,
Williamsburg, Virginia

2. Nancy Ross Wilson, *Westward the Women* (San Francisco, CA: North Point, 1985), 174.

3. For illustrations of family record and genealogy samplers, see Betty Ring, *American Needlework Treasures* (New York: Dutton, 1987), 14–17.

4. Illustrated and discussed in Gloria Seaman Allen, *First Flowerings: Early Virginia Quilts* (Washington, DC: DAR Museum, 1987), 30. Allen suggests the quiltmaker's marriage to Samuel Chewning the following year may have brought an end to her work on this memorial piece.

5. 1850 census records confirm these relationships. Emily's age is 45, and her property is listed at $1,600. Her surviving children still reside with her; Lafayette's occupation is listed as "Butcher." The extended family includes Emily A. Vandegrift (age 13, she attended school, as did Benjamin, George, and Howard); Rebecca Vandegrift, age 82; Caroline Strickland, age 33; and John Sharp, a 65-year-old black man with no listed profession, and whom the census taker noted could neither read nor write. Several Vandegrifts signed the surrounding signature blocks, as did young Emily.

6. The other three inscriptions: "The fear of the Lord is a / fountain of life, to depart from / the snares of death.," "The fear of the Lord is the / beginning of wisdom: which will / lead us to forsake sin.," and "The fear of the Lord is a strong / confidence; and his children / shall have a place of refu[g]e."

153. The Dear Little Charlie Quilt
Made by Jennette Crossman Evans
Rock County, Wisconsin
Circa 1870
73¼ x 80 in. (186 x 203.2 cm)
Los Angeles County Museum of Art, gift of
Richard and Cynthia Jones

Dear Little Charlie

The tragic realities of infant mortality in the early nineteenth century were carved on stones throughout the eastern states, and embroidered on the tombs worked on mourning pictures by such refined young ladies as Harriot Amanda Burgess (1800–70), a student at Miss Balch's School in Providence, Rhode Island.[1] Harriot's memorial (no. 154) is done in silk and silk chenille with watercolor on a satin-weave silk ground, and the tomb on the left is dedicated to two of her brothers, who died young:

> Consecrated / to / the memory / of / JOB M. BURGESS, / who was born April 19, 1802, / and died May 16th, 1802. / aged 27 days. / And / BENJAMIN B. BURGESS, / who was born October 23rd, 1803. / and departed this life May 3rd, 1806. / aged 2 years and 7 months.

> Grieve not fond Parents at thy infants doom, / Early their path was open'd to the tomb, / Early, to thee they bade a last adieu, / And closed their eyes upon this earth and you.[2]

Sarah Connell Ayer (a New England quiltmaker who had written earlier of happier moments, quilting together with family and friends: "In the afternoon Susan Ayer and myself went down to assist Susan Gale in quilting. We had a fine frolic . . . "[3]) wrote in 1815 of this resignation to the death of her young children:

> September 29th. 1815. . . . Since closing my last journal [26 October 1811], I have been the mother of four children, which now lay side by side in the grave-yard. The first was born in <u>1811, Dec. 10th</u>. The second the <u>10th of Oct. 1812</u>, and lived only two days, the third the <u>4th</u> of <u>Sept. 1813</u>, and the <u>4th</u>. the <u>25th of Nov. 1814</u>. This last was a sweet, interesting boy, and lived to be six months old. He was a lovely flower, and I trust he is now transplanted in the garden of Heaven. Though the death of this child was a great trial, yet I hope I was made to bow submissive to the will of my Heavenly Father.[4]

The comforting thought of immortality for her own two precious lost boys, safe in that "garden of Heaven," was also written in ink on the small centers of two of the flower-like motifs that comprised the surface of Jennette Evans's mourning quilt (no. 154):

154. Burgess Memorial (detail)
Harriot Amanda Burgess
Providence, Rhode Island
Possibly 1819
20¹⁄₁₆ x 24¹⁄₁₆ in. (51 x 61.1 cm)
Abby Aldrich Rockefeller Folk Art Center, Williamsburg, Virginia

Dear little Charlie / died Oct 28th 1852 / Aged two years and / six months. / — / The grave is not my / loved ones home (no. 155)

Dear Little Franky, / died Jan 19th 1855. / Aged three years, / — / He is an angel / now. (no. 156)

These sad inscriptions flank yet a third (no. 157), "In memory / of / Robert L. Evans. / My dear husband / who died Jan 23rd / 1865. There is rest for the weary." Elsewhere on the quilt, another is dedicated to "My Robert. / I will meet thee in / Heaven" (no. 158), and the fabric from which those outer hexagons are constructed is one that might well have been used for a gentleman's vest. We do not know the extent of Jennette's production of clothing for Robert, and indeed it may have only extended to the plain sewing of shirts and pants, but the letters and journals of others often suggest a wife's particular pleasure in having sewn some special bit of finery for her husband. (In Maria Langworthy Whitford's diary, for example, among multiple mentions of "quiltings"[5] in her rural western New York community, she noted having "Done housework and commenced to spin some lammas fur to make Sam'l an overcoat."[6] "Cut out a pair of pants for Sam'l out of some beaver satinett,"[7] and "Knit on a fur mitten for Sam'l."[8] She records the making or mending of a vest on half a dozen occasions, including that "white vest for Sam'l."[9]

In the middle of the century, we know that in the concept of "quilting together" a valued contribution of labor was not always in the form of tight, even little running stitches at a "merry quilting," but often only in the construction of a single block to be

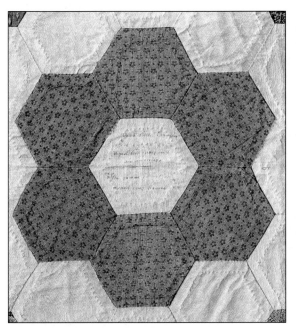

155. The Dear Little Charlie Quilt (detail)

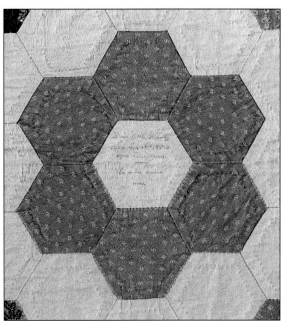

156. The Dear Little Charlie Quilt (detail)

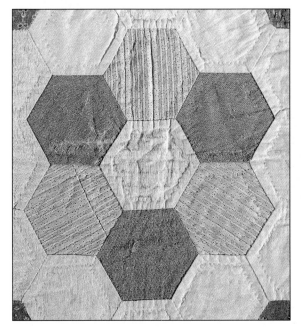

157. The Dear Little Charlie Quilt (detail)

158. The Dear Little Charlie Quilt (detail)

159. The Album Patch Quilt
      Maker unidentified
      Probably Connecticut
      Circa 1860
      92⅜ x 94¼ in. (234.6 x 239.4 cm)
      Darwin D. Bearley Antiques, Akron, Ohio

contributed to the whole. The use of fabrics that would serve as reminders of the family and friends from whose clothing they came was noted in *Godey's Lady's Book* in February 1857: "An old lady, an aunt of mine, one of the single sisterhood, is constantly making the most beautiful patchwork quilts. She has one made entirely of pieces of dresses worn by the different members of the family. This is her family quilt, and it really seems odd to see so many familiar pieces made into one article."[10] Those "familiar pieces" were most often printed cottons contained in such simple pieced quilts. In one such memory (nos. 159 and 160), multiple signed blocks include one small memorial inscription: "Adeline L. Whitney / Who died aged 5 years," and many bearing locations as well: New Haven and Colebrook, Connecticut; Landsfield and Sheffield. Twenty of the seventy-three individuals named on Jennette's quilt have been identified as relatives or their spouses;[11] Jennette (born 20 May 1824, died 23 January 1875) was the daughter of Warren Crossman and Susan B. Clapp and married Robert Evans on 31 December 1845, and the names of Cro[f]sman, Clapp, and Evans abound on her quilt. Their contribution to her "quilting" may have come only in the form of additional hexagonal "blocks" or bits of fabric.

Jennette included other memorial inscriptions that in addition to that made from Robert's vest are in all probability constructed from clothing of those deceased, including "Nancy Fowler. / Died in 1843" (no. 161), "The Memory of the just and the blefsed / Grandmother Crofsman / died in 1855," "Susan D. Crofsman. / my dear mother" (no. 162), and most tenderly, "Gone but not forgotten. / Lucy M. Truesdell, / died in March 1854. / My dear sister" (no. 163). In New England young Lucy Larcom was similarly moved by the sight of a bit of cotton cloth:

160. The Album Patch Quilt (detail)

I liked assorting those little figured bits of cotton cloth, for they were scraps of gowns I had seen worn, and they reminded me of the persons who wore them. One fragment, in particular, was like a picture to me. It was a delicate pink and brown sea-moss pattern, on a white ground, a piece of a dress belonging to my married sister, who was to me bride and angel in one. I always saw her face before me when I unfolded this scrap .... Heaven claimed her before my childhood was ended. Her beautiful form was laid to rest in mid-ocean, too deep to be pillowed among the soft sea-mosses.[12]

At ages two and three, dear little Charlie and dear little Franky may still have worn dresses and the two somewhat-worn turkey

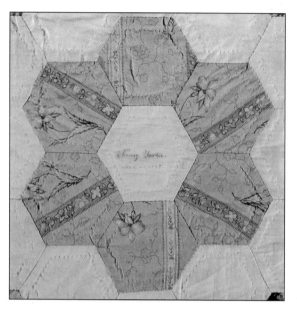

161. The Dear Little Charlie Quilt (detail)

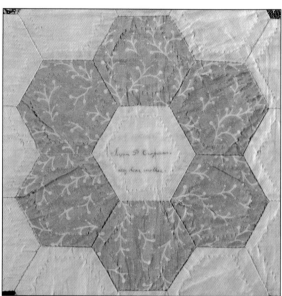

162. The Dear Little Charlie Quilt (detail)

red fabrics that hold their memorials may well have evoked the most poignant memories of all.

The wish to gather those lingering remembrances was in the Victorian tradition of mourning, not unlike the wish to secure a photographic image of the dead child prepared for the grave.

> The flowers A[melia] J[ane] sent in her first letter after I came out, I pinned on our darling's breast with the little breast pin her cousin Mattie C. gave her. She was dressed to look as natural as possible, lying a little on one side with her doll Aunt Mary gave her in her arms just as when she went to sleep . . . I can't fully realize I won't see her here any more. (July 3, 1886)[13]

Others were photographed held awkwardly in the arms of a grieving parent, but more often the children were shown as if safely asleep in their beds, or on a couch, often with flowers held in their tiny hands (no. 164). They were, like dear little Franky, "an angel now."

NOTES

1. *American Folk Paintings: Paintings and Drawings Other Than Portraits from the Abby Aldrich Rockefeller Folk Art Center.* The Abby Aldrich Rockefeller Folk Art Center Series, edited by Beatrice T. Rumford, no. 2. (Boston: Little, Brown, 1988), 403. The definitive work on such schools and schoolmistresses is Betty Ring, *Girlhood Embroidery: American Samplers & Pictorial Needlework 1650–1850* (New York: Knopf, 1993).
2. To the right of the children's tomb, a small mourner kneels before the primary monument, inscribed to Harriot's mother: "Consecrated to the remains / of / Mrs. ABIGAIL BURGESS, / consort of Mr. Benjamin Burgess, who died / Sept. 17th, 1811. in the 43rd year of her age." and "Her tranquil soul has took its flight,/ To that immortal rest — / Where troubles cease, and sorrows end, / Within her peaceful breast."

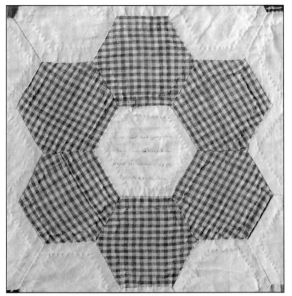 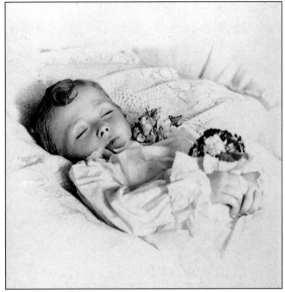

163. The Dear Little Charlie Quilt (detail}

164. Undated photograph
Tekamah, Nebraska
Private Collection

3. Sarah Connell Ayer, *Diary of Sarah Connell Ayer* (Portland, ME: Lefavor-Tower, 1910), 126.
4. Ibid., 209.
5. Maria Langworthy Whitford, — *And a White Vest for Sam'l: An Account of Rural Life in Western N.Y. from the diaries of Maria Langworthy Whitford of Alfred Station, N.Y. 1857–1861*, Helene C. Phelan, ed., (Alfred, NY: Sun, 1976). In 1857, for example: "October 22nd. I done up the work and got ready to go down to Uncle E.'s to help them quilt on Amanda's quilt. Helped get the quilt on and quilted till night. October 25th. . . . done up work, went down to Uncle Ezra's to help them quilt in the afternoon. October 28th. Done up the work early and went down to help quilt. November 5th. Went to Uncle Ezra to help them quilt on Amanda's bed quilt all day."
6. Ibid., 31.
7. Ibid., 39.
8. Ibid., 45.
9. Ibid., 134.
10. Ellen Lindsay, "Patchwork," *Godey's Lady's Book and Magazine* (February 1857), 166.
11. Memorandum, Rick J. Ashton, The Newberry Library, Chicago (5 October 1976).
12. Lucy Larcom, *A New England Girlhood: Outlined From Memory* (Boston: Houghton, Mifflin, 1892), 122–23.
13. Byrd Gibbens, "Charles and Maggie Brown in Colorado and New Mexico. 1880–1930" in *Far from Home: Families of the Westward Journey* (New York: Schocken, 1989), 153.

165. The Spiritualists Quilt Top
Highland County, Virginia
Circa 1857
81 x 56½ in. (205.7 x 142.9 cm)
Los Angeles County Museum of Art,
American Quilt Research Center Acquisition Fund

When Next You Come Who Will You Be

Early quiltmakers' letters and diaries speak often of "circles," and of the comfort and continuity they provided. Sarah Connell Ayer, living at various times in Massachusetts, New Hampshire, and Maine, commented frequently on the pleasure of quilting with others: "This forenoon we put in the quilt, and this afternoon Mrs. Thomson, Mrs. Storer and Miss. Gott came to assist us. We had a fine time, and were all cheerful." (25 July 1810),[1] and of the circle of family and friends that provided an important framework for her domestic contentment:

> We set around the blazing hearth sweet sociability prevails, and cheerfulness smiles throughout our little circle. May the angel of domestic peace hover over our dwelling.[2]

> I felt a kind of pensive pleasure, in looking round on the little circle, and felt an ardent desire to make my family happy, and our dwelling the seat of domestic peace, virtue and religion.[3]

"Domestic peace, virtue, and religion" were of course her responsibility (and would increasingly be so as gender played an ever more prominent role in society's assignment of specific and separate spheres). But also within those circles: "We danced, then play'd, and the most cheerful good humour prevail'd throughout our little circle,"[4] and "On our return I sang several favourite songs to entertain our little circle of happy friends, they were gratified and I was happy."[5] Such quiltmakers as Sarah and her friends and family were also responsible for the plain and fancy sewing within their households, and for the production of clothing as well, and when not at their quilting frames a sewing basket might well hold a variety of small bits of work to be done: "This afternoon we all took our work and sat down in the common setting-room. Sweet sociability prevail'd throughout our little [sewing] circle, and we were all satisfied with ourselves and happy in each other."[6]

The "circles" of which Sarah and others wrote frequently overlapped, and contracted and expanded. The circle might be broken in a number of ways, and when departure or death disrupted the constancy of those relationships, the loss was profoundly lamented.

This was confirmed on 7 January 1791, in a letter written by Peggy White Bartlett to Elizabeth Cranch, then living in Weymouth, Massachusetts:

> You wished me to let you know a little of our circle of acquaintances which we had in the year [17]'86. I scarcely know how to begin. They are dispersed from one part of the globe to the other and some alas! are no more. . . . Mr. Tyler is gone to the Ohio! and poor Flint is no more. . . . I wish you were here to join in some of our circles. I do long to talk over some of our times which are past.
> Adieu, Adieu   thine P.B.[7]

And half a century later, written on a delicately embellished silk block (no. 166):

> Hannah M. Morris.
> The circle is broken — one seat is forsaken

166. The Quaker Memorial Quilt (detail)
Pennsylvania or New Jersey
Marked 1850
118 x 132½ in. (299.7 x 336.6 cm)
Los Angeles County Museum of Art, Costume Council Fund

One bud from the tree of our friendship is shaken,
One heart from among us no longer shall thrill,
With the spirit of gladnefs, or darken with ill.

There were other circles at work by the middle of the nineteenth century, Spiritualists seated not around a quilting frame but around a table, hands touching, hoping to call up that clouded image or muffled voice that might once again close the circle (no. 167).

There is reference to an intense interest or participation in the occult, and later in Spiritualism, in a substantial number of quiltmakers' diaries and journals, including many of those quoted in this publication. Visiting in Haverhill in 1785, for example, Elizabeth Cranch was "much amazed there with a fortune telling skreen,"[8] and in 1797, at Hillsborough, young Frances Baylor Hill "got up early broke an egg in a glass of water, but was sadly disappoint'd at not seeing anything of consequence in it."[9] Similarly, Jesse Applegate remembered that during his journey to Oregon in 1843, "Some girl cousins, older

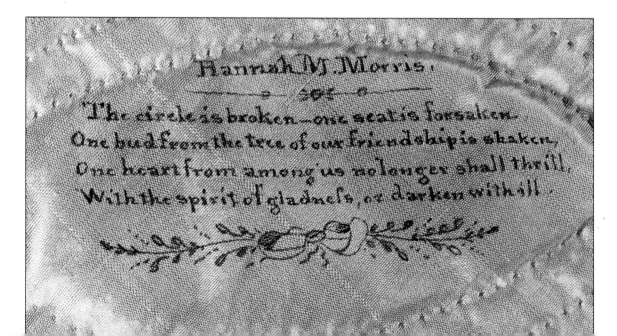

167. Illustration, *The Phenomenon of Table-Moving* From Andrew Jackson Davis, *The Present Age and Inner Life; Ancient and Modern Spirit Mysteries Classified and Explained* (Boston: William White, 1870), unpaginated

168. Book covers. Left: *Mesmerism Mind Reading Hypnotism and Spiritualism: How to Hypnotize* (Chicago: M.A. Donohue & Co., n.d.) and Right: *Comforts Palmistry Guide by Chiero the Palmist: "The Tell Tale Hand"* (n.p., n.d.) Private Collection

than I, would take a coffee cup after drinking the coffee, and turn the mouth down, and after it had set a short time, look into it for pictures of future scenes."[10] Lucy Larcom remembered "an earnest Christian woman, of keen intelligence and unusual spiritual perception. She was supposed by her neighbors to have the gift of "second sight," and "some remarkable stories are told of her knowledge of distant events while they were occurring, or just before they took place."[11] In 1857, Abigail Malick's son-in-law had consulted "Mrs. Vauliou the Astrologist" to give him a vision of the future. "She said that my boy was very sick. She showed me [his] sweet Likeness

through an instrument. I could see him as plane as life & pale as death."[12]

Spiritualists seem to have abounded in Lynn, Massachusetts (see "Woman's Work Is Never Done"). Two and a half weeks before the dedication of the Boston Street Methodist Church in 1853, John Hutchinson, a poet and vocalist, was buried from his stone cottage at High Rock. "He was a spiritualist, and, it is said, pledged himself to return, after entering the spirit land, and convince mankind of the truth of his views. But for some cause, he appears to have failed in fulfilling his pledge."[13] And nine years later, "a grand picnic party under the auspices of the Spiritualists, was held at Dungeon Rock. Some two thousand persons of both sexes and all ages were present. There was speaking, music, and dancing. Mediums were in attendance, and divers revelations made. The day was pleasant, and the proceedings went forward with spirit."[14]

The modern Spiritualism movement is generally regarded to have begun in Hydesville, Wayne County, New York, in 1848 with supposedly unexplained rappings in the home of two young sisters, Kate and Margaret Fox, the knocking said to be produced by spirits wishing to communicate. Kate and Margaret offered themselves as the first "mediums," links between the living and the dead. In addition to the soon-coded rappings and moving furniture, seances began to produce spirit lights, luminous hands, faces, and figures in which the participants might recognize a loved one, sometimes speaking to them from beyond the grave through the "medium" that had drawn them all together. The movement spread rapidly throughout the Western world, converting not only the uneducated but extending into the intellectual community as well. Spiritualism's popularity was manifested in the pamphlets in believers' parlors (no. 168) and on advertisements for the soap on their pantry shelves (no. 169).

It would seem unlikely that quiltmakers were absent from the vast numbers of Spiritualist circles in the second half of the nineteenth century. Their presence is made known, in fact, by a unique quilt top (no. 165), poorly constructed and awkwardly assembled, but bearing several inscriptions that the author finds difficult to interpret otherwise. Two inscriptions (no. 170) seem most conclusive: "When next you come who will you be," and "Laura you'll return to us 'information.'"

"Spirit circles" formed within many families, and the names on this quilt top confirm that it was indeed that overlapping family circle within which this enigmatic object was worked. Thirty-one pieced blocks[15] surround a larger, appliquéd panel. Twenty-seven are signed, and of those the majority bear dates and/or geographic locations, and from that information, these things are known: the signatures were probably secured between 1853

169. Undated trade card, "Kendall Mfg Co. Providence, R.I."
Private Collection

and 1857 (of the later dates on the blocks, three were signed on February 4, one on March 7, and two on October 28, and eight were signed 1853, four of those specifically on April 15); the members of the circle (whose surnames are Campbell, Hull, Lindsey, McClung, Patt[erse?]n, Rexroad, Sitlington, Slaven, Sterret, Wilson, and Woods) all seem to have lived in, or close to, Highland County, Virginia, specifically Crab Bottom, Highland, McDowell, Meadow Dale, Mount Airy, Mountain View, and Woodlawn; and all were intermingled by birth or by marriage.

If those facts are known, the specific incident that prompted the project and the

170. The Spiritualists Quilt Top (detail)

person whose passing seems to have inspired it remains elusive. From Sallie Hull's instruction to "Laura" we might reasonably assume it was she. Research to date has found several family members named Laura, but none whose date of death fits within the dates the inscriptions have established. The instigator of this undertaking may have been Nannie S. Sterrett,[16] who signed one of the pieced blocks and who signed, and perhaps appliquéd, the rather incongruous, bow-tied, floral wreath, on the central panel (no. 171). On that larger block she seems to confirm that Laura was a "friend": "For my friend / who I hope to see again / Gone but not forever." (A dear friend was often called "sister," but it is unlikely a sister would have been referred to as a friend.) It may be significant that the three women who signed blocks with specifically Spiritualistic messages —Sallie Hull, Nannie Sterrett, and Mary Rexroad ("Come back to us.") — are the three who also indicated they lived in McDowell, Highland County, Virginia. Perhaps that was Laura's earthly home as well.

171. The Spiritualists Quilt Top (detail)

NOTES

1. Sarah Connell Ayer, *Diary of Sarah Connell Ayer* (Portland, ME: Lefavor-Tower, 1910), 167.
2. Ibid., 31. Sarah perceived that "domestic peace" hovering over other dwellings also: "We past several little cottages, the lights of which, showed us their situation. My busy imagination pictured the happy circle round the rustic supper, each partaking his homely fare. Here, methought is contentment. The happy family wish for nothing beyond what their little affords.," 42.
3. Ibid., 207. During this period, a reference to "family" would often include all members of the household, not only those bound by birth or marriage. For Sarah, "our little family consist[ed] of Mr. Ayer and myself, Aunt Newman, Mary Greenleaf, and Woodbury Hatch, a boy about 13 years that we have taken to live with us."
4. Ibid., 11.
5. Ibid., 167.
6. Ibid., 164.
7. Lizzie Norton Mason and James Duncan Phillips, eds. "The Journal of Elizabeth Cranch." *Essex Institute Historical Collections* 80 (1944), 4.
8. Ibid., p. 8.
9. Frances Baylor Hill, "The Diary of Frances Baylor Hill of 'Hillsborough,' King and Queen County, Virginia" (1797). Edited by William K. Bottorff and Roy C. Flannagan. *Early American Literature Newsletter* 3 (Winter 1967), 26.
10. Jesse Applegate, *Recollections of My Boyhood* (Roseburg, OR: Press of Review Publishing, 1914), 9.
11. Lucy Larcom, *A New England Girlhood: Outlined from Memory* (Boston: Houghton, Mifflin, 1892), 20.
12. Quoted in Lillian Schlissel, "The Malick Family in Oregon Territory" in *Far from Home: Families of the Westward Journey* (New York: Schocken, 1989), 64.
13. Alonzo Lewis and James R. Newhall, *History of Lynn, Essex County, Massachusetts* (Boston: John L. Shorey, 1865), 437.
14. Ibid., 471.
15. The signed squares of muslin may have been expanded into the full blocks by a hand or hands other than the signatories, and at a somewhat later date.
16. Nancy Snyder Sitlington Sterrett (Nannie) was born in Crab Bottom, Virginia, in 1833; her mother died ten days later. She married Robert Dunlap Sterrett in 1850, and they lived together near the Rockridge Baths where their son John was born in 1851 and where Robert died the following year. (As an adult, John Robert Sitlington Sterrett was a distinguished archaeologist and university professor. *Who Was Who in America*, Vol. I, 1897–1942, 1179.) Nannie married John William P. Alexander in 1856; they had nine children. John W. Sitlington ("When next you come who will you be") was Nannie's uncle; when his block was signed, he was living just north of McDowell in Crab Bottom, Virginia, where Nannie Sterrett had been born.

When Thou Art Gone to Western Land

*I*n 1836, George and Abigail Malick and their four young children moved by wagon from Sunbury, Pennsylvania, to Tazewell County, Illinois, and twelve years later they left Illinois in another wagon with six children (Charles, Hiram, Rachel, Peter, Abigail Jane, and Nancy), bound for Oregon Territory. They had left behind their eldest daughter, pregnant with her fourth child, and unless Mary Ann and her husband could somehow be persuaded to join them later, Abigail acknowledged in a letter the probable permanence of their separation: "I never shal see eney of you eny More in this world." (10 October 1850).[1]

It was the letters Abigail Malick wrote, and those she hoped to receive, that she determined would keep her family somehow bound together, and they were not unlike those between other families caught up and torn apart as America moved West. In 1852, after a "wearisome journey" to Sacramento, Elizabeth Keegan wrote to her brother and sister back in Missouri, "If I was back in St Louis now, I would not come here. . . ."[2] She was twelve years old, riding her pony, and accompanied only by her mother, a servant girl named Kate, and a hired man, and it was a particularly tragic year on the Overland Trail. "There was but one graveyard that hot, dusty, dreadful year of 1852, and that graveyard reached from the Missouri to the Columbia."[3] Elizabeth and her small party escaped the "Aseatic Cholera in its worst form from the beginning to the end of the journey,"[4] but once they had reached California, another peril seemed to have loomed large. "Mother particularly requests that you both write the 1st and 15th of every month without fail if you wish to keep her alive until she sees you both again."[5]

The Malick letters were filled with common news and uncommon grief, and sent with photographs, seeds, and bits of cloth. Rachel married and, settling into remembered rituals, began attending "grand quiltens" with as many as "15 ladeys."[6] She sent a snip of baby Charley's hair and a swatch of satin from his bonnet.[7] "[I made] myself a brown Meerino dress and I will put up a peice of it in this letter" (10 October 1853).[8] Abigail promised to send some samples of calico "so you Can se what sort of Cloaths we ware in Oregon."[9] Those bits of cloth marked life's cycles: in telling Mary Ann of their father's death, Rachel promised that their mother would send "some of our morning dresses and some of his shroud"

172. The Elsie Ann Burr Quilt
    Made by Elsie Ann Burr
    Fairfield, Illinois
    Marked 1849
    83 x 67 in. (210.6 x 170.2 cm)
    Los Angeles County Museum of Art, gift of
    Patricia Burr (Mrs. Jackson) Edwards

(29 October 1854),[10] and in January 1857, Abigail sent a bit of blue silk from Abigail Jane's wedding dress.[11]

Atwell and Betsey Wheeler Burr had also moved to Illinois in 1836, traveling from Pompey, New York, with their nine children to settle in St. Charles, Kane County. In 1849, when she was twenty-five years old, their daughter Elsie Ann returned to upper New York State to visit the family and friends they had left behind. And it was bits of cloth she also craved.

She was only eleven years old when she left Pompey, and for Elsie Ann these must have been grand reunions. Wherever she visited, she requested pieces of cotton dresses and shirts to carry back to Fairfield, Illinois, to be marked for an album quilt (no. 172): from "Little Flora D.," for example, and cousins Betsey, Elnora, Frizah, and Sarah Ann in Pompey; Aunt Eunita, and cousins Frances and Lovantia in DeRuyter. Worked by several hands, the names would eventually number forty, including her own (no. 173), from more than a dozen small New York villages. It is one other name from DeRuyter that may have determined the off-sided placement of the red cross-stitched inscriptions. As on almost all the other blocks, the name and village, "Cousin S. Lavonia R / DeRuyter," have been entered on the right-hand side of the strip of muslin but here to the left has also been entered: "Died March 5th 49 / Aged 18. / She lives again/ in Heaven" (no. 174). Perhaps the open spaces on the others were intended to be inscribed eventually with their own inevitable dates of death.

Abigail Malick had also rendered death notices, not in tiny, tidy little crossed stitches, but in ragged letters on the pages of those years of letters from Oregon. The first, and the hardest, spoke of the loss of her seventeen-year-old son, Hiram, dead just three months after their journey had begun. In a

173. The Elsie Ann Burr Quilt (detail)

174. The Elsie Ann Burr Quilt (detail)

letter to Mary Ann, she described at length how "Hiram drounded in [the] Plat River At the Mouth of Dear Krick":

So you know All about Hiram's death now. So you need not ask eneything

About him eney More for it will not do us eney Good to trouble ourselves About him eney More. It has Almost kild Me but I have to bear it. And if we Are good perhapes then we can meete him in heven (10 October1850).[12]

Showing an even earlier propensity for expressions of mourning, Elsie Ann Burr had also put pen to paper in "LINES, / Composed on the Death of DANIEL WARNE, / who died January 7th, 1843, in the / twenty-fourth year of his age" (no. 175). But for her quilt, Elsie Ann, who never married, incorporated the needlework skills she had refined in Pompey, the same letters and basket she had learned as a young girl on

> Miss Elsie Ann. Burr,s Sampler (no. 176)
> Wrought in the 11th year of her age
> While under the instruction of L. Cobb
> Pompey August the 10 1835.

Even in 1855, Illinois still held the promise of cheap land, and with his older brother Charles having already taken his assumed place on their father's prosperous New Jersey farm, it was Alexander Hoagland's intention that following their wedding he and his young bride should move to Jerseyville, Illinois, to join those other New Jersey pioneers who had already settled the area. Alexander was twenty-eight and Cornelia only twenty,[13] and they carried with them a bright, sturdy cotton quilt (nos. 177 and 178) bearing the names and sentiments of family and friends and surely intended, particularly for Cornelia, to soften the emotional journey: "We have been friends together / It cannot all be over / We will be friends forever / Though here we meet no more" Jane Suydam / February 27, 1855[14] (no. 179).

Helen Gulick wrote tenderly of the imminent departure (no. 180):

LINES,

Composed on the Death of DANIEL WARNE, who died January 7th, 1843, in the twenty-fourth year of his age.

BY MISS E. A. BURR.

Ye weeping friends with me draw near,
And pause o'er him who slumbers here,
Though cold his form beneath the sod,
His spirit winged its way to God.

By all beloved—in prime of life,   [rife,
What though his thoughts with hopes were
Consumption came, and none could save
Its victim from an early grave.

His friends were many, foes were few,
For every one his kindness knew,
And many plead with fervent prayer,
That death would still their idol spare.

How brightly beamed his rising sun,
How cheerful sped his moments on,
And even on the couch of pain
His cheerfulness was still the same.

And did his spirit quake with fear
When last the solemn hour drew near?
Ah! no; he calmly, sweetly said,
" My friends, approach my dying bed;

Farewell, dear father—mother, too;
And brothers, sisters—all adieu.
I pray you do not weep for me,
For you can spare me now," said he.

" Kind Heaven decrees it must be so,
And I am willing now to go;
One parting kiss, and then I die,
And leave this world without a sigh."

How keen the woe for friends most true,
To give that long, that last adieu.
He's gone—but aye, he's freed from pain,
Their loss is his eternal gain.

Dry, dry your tears; he's gone above,
Where all is joy, and peace, and love,
With angels in that blest abode,
He chants the praises of his God.

175. Published poem by Elsie Ann Burr
Unidentified source
1843

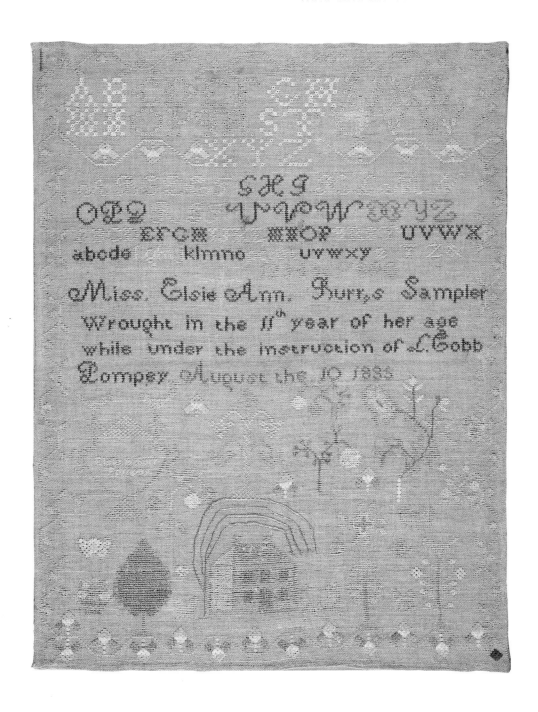

176. Sampler
Made by Elsie Ann Burr
Pompey, New York
Marked 10 August 1835
21¾ x 17 in. (55.3 x 43.1 cm)
Los Angeles County Museum of Art, gift of
Patricia Burr (Mrs. Jackson) Edwards

177. The Hoagland Quilt
    Made for Alexander Hoagland and Cornelia
    Baird Hoagland
    South Brunswick Township, Middlesex
    County, New Jersey
    Marked 1855
    90⅛ x 81 in. (228.9 x 205.7 cm)
    Los Angeles County Museum of Art, gift of
    Herbert L. Wallerstein Jr.

178. The Hoagland Quilt (detail)

179. The Hoagland Quilt (detail)

Oh when thou art gone to Western land,
And dream of friends away,
And visions of thine eastern home
Around thee sadly play,
Then fondly look upon these names
That friendships hand may trace
And solaced by thier memory niece
To sad regrets give place,

as did Fannie V. King:

The gay Savannah's of the West,
Are soon to be thy home,
The dear wild bird we loved so well
Will from us widely roam
But when at night you bend the knee
Unto your childhood's God
Oh! let us then remembered be
Whose name we here record.

Fannie's reference to remembrance at the time of evening prayer ("when at night you bend the knee") is a phrase used frequently, in multiple variations. An earlier New Jersey inscription (Plainfield, 1848) appears on a quilt presented to Jane and Elias Randolph for their journey to Wisconsin:

180. The Hoagland Quilt (detail)

Whene'er you think on those away,
And when you bend the pious knee,
Or when your thoughts to pleasure stray
Oh then, dear Jane, remember me,[15]

and another is inscribed on one of four pieced blocks joined together (no. 181):

181. Four joined quilt blocks (detail)
     Blocks signed by Susanna D. Dennis and
     Sarah Murphy
     United States
     Marked March 4th 1844
     20 x 20 in. (50.8 x 50.8 cm)
     Abby Aldrich Rockefeller Folk Art Center,
     Williamsburg, Virginia

182a. and 182b. Undated letter. Princeton, New
     Jersey

Remmember me when thou doth sigh
And softly bend the knee
To ofer up thy prayer on high
Oh then remember me.
Susanna D. Dennis / March 4th 1844 /
Roseville.

A mid-twentieth-century letter (nos. 182a
and 182b) attached to Cornelia's mid-nine-
teenth-century quilt is a reasonably accurate,
if somewhat   romantically embellished, family remembrance:

Album Quilt.
     As dates on the quilt show it was
made in 1855. Each block was made by
the friend who signed it. This was put
together and quilted to be taken to the
new home of Cornelia Baird Hoagland
in Jerseyville, Illinois.
     Cornelia Baird lived in Ten Mile
Run New Jersey. She was the daughter
of Benjamin and Susan Baird. As a girl
she fell violently in love with Alexander
Hoagland from the same village. Their
courtship was a violent and sweet affair.
Truly a "He loves me," "He loves me
not" courtship. Alexander decided it all

by arranging to go to Illinois. They were engaged, married and off in the shortest possible time.

The married life of these two was short, short but breath takingly happy. Less than a year after they were married Cornelia took a fever and passed on.

Alexander wrote the homefolks the details of their happiness. In words that said in substance, "we lived a century of happiness in this one year." He sent Cornelia's most intimate possessions to her mother. These included fourteen good silk dresses, twenty-one petticoats and this quilt.

The quilt was stored in a trunk in an attic. The roof leaked and stained the quilt but neither weather nor time can change the happiness the quilt brought two New Jersey lovers as they journied to their new home in Illinois.

As Abigail Malick had written of her hope to see her dear "drounded" Hiram again, across the continent Abigail Cox prophetically inscribed on her block (no. 183) to that "dear wild bird,"

May we meet in heaven.

183. The Hoagland Quilt (detail)

NOTES

1. Quoted in Lillian Schlissel, "The Malick Family in Oregon Territory" in *Far from Home: Families of the Westward Journey* (New York: Schocken, 1989), 10. The Malick Family Correspondence, 1848–69, is in the Beinecke Library at Yale University. All material used by the author from these remarkable letters is quoted in Schlissel's exemplary interpretive segment in *Far from Home.*
2. Quoted in Kenneth L. Holmes, ed., *Covered Wagon Women: Diaries & Letters from the Western Trails 1840–1890,* Vol. IV (Glendale, CA: Arthur H. Clark, 1985), 28.
3. Joaquin Miller. From an unnamed newspaper, 1905. Quoted in Holmes, *Covered Wagon Women,* 13. Miller, a noted California poet, had crossed the plains as a teenager in 1852.
4. Holmes, *Covered Wagon Women,* 24.
5. Holmes, *Covered Wagon Women,* 30.
6. Schlissel, "The Malick Family," 27.
7. Schlissel, "The Malick Family," 28-29.
8. Schlissel, "The Malick Family," 35.
9. Schlissel, "The Malick Family," 39.
10. Schlissel, "The Malick Family," 40.
11. Schlissel, "The Malick Family," 59. (Additional information on Jane Malick is found on pp. 143–44 of this book.)
12. Schlissel, "The Malick Family," 10.
13. Based on the 1850 United States census records for Middlesex County, New Jersey.
14. The reassurance of the constancy of friendship in the face of separation is a continuing theme on such quilts. "If while on earth we have to part — / And move to far off distant lands, / If friendship has entwined the heart, / Distance can never break the bands" was inscribed on a quilt block in 1856 by William C. Richardson, Randolph, Vermont. Collection of the Randolph Historical Society and illustrated in Richard L. Cleveland and Donna Bister, *Plain and Fancy: Vermont's People and Their Quilts As a Reflection of America* (Gualala, CA: Quilt Digest Press, 1991), 55.
15. Jean Ray Laury, *Ho for California! Pioneer Women and Their Quilts* (New York: Dutton, 1990), 29.

184. The Asylum Quilt
Made by inmates of the Salt Lake City
Insane Asylum
Salt Lake City, Utah
Circa 1880
73 x 73½ in. (185.4 x 186.7 cm)
Courtesy Museum of Church History and
Art, Salt Lake City, Utah

I Think I Will Sirtenly Get Insane

In Oregon in 1859, Abigail Malick's energy and expectations were gone.

> I Am Tierd of Being here And Haveing So Mutch Trouble About Every Thing About this Land. And Loosing so Meny of My Familey has put me almost Besid My Self. Some Times I Think I Sirtenly Will get Insane.[1]

But it was her nineteen-year-old daughter, Jane, who went mad.

> She distrois All that Come Before Her When She Has Her Crasy Spells on her And Wantes to kill All Derest Frendes And her Little Babe.[2]

Abigail admitted in a letter to her family in Illinois that she had been compelled to take Jane's baby from her for two and three days at a time "And tie her down on the Bed and it took Three of us to do it At that. So you May think I Have Had a hard time of it with her."[3] When the situation became increasingly public (Jane had gone outside to the well, stripped herself nude to the waist, scoured herself with a black boll brush and sand, and then climbed to the top of the house and begun to pull the shingles from the roof and tear the top off the chimney), it was Abigail's great fear that

> We Shuld Have Had to of sent her to Stockton [California] to the mad House or the Insane Ascilum. And that would Have Bin very hard for Her And us. For They Whip them Every Morning or When they do Eny thing, so I am told, And get hardley Eny thing to Eat.[4]

Jane had been pregnant out of wedlock, entered into an unstable marriage, lost her first baby, and been abandoned by her husband. For other women in the West, especially those on the prairie, it was often assumed simply to have been the endless wind and solitude that drove them mad. But whatever the causes, insanity was a presence that could not be ignored and asylums were among those public buildings taking shape on the western frontier. As they camped on a hill in Page County, Iowa, Viola Springer noted in her 1885 diary, "The state is building an asylum in Clarinda, begun it this spring. They intend to build one-fourth of it this season. They say it will take them 7 years to get it completed."[5] On 27 May 1879, crossing Iowa to file for land under the Nebraska Homestead Act, Ada Colvin "Saw the Insane

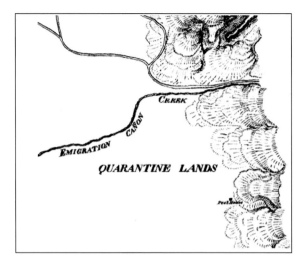

185. Map, "Salt Lake City and Vicinity, Utah"
(detail),
Browne and Brooks, 20 February 1888
Courtesy Utah State Historical Society

Asylum just west of Independence. Large Building can be seen for miles."[6] (Ada's own depression is established by the diary begun before she left Whitewater, Wisconsin: "Arthur [her brother] died at five this morning, very easy. Why is it if I care for anything or anyone it is either taken from me or leaves me. . . . He is out of this world of sin and misery. God knows I wish I laid beside free from all trouble and sorrow."[7] Six months later, camping near the Platte River, Ada wrote in her diary " Arthur's birthday. . . . tonight I'm sitting with a bed quilt around my chest, hat on my head playing dice with Fred. Such is Western life. Wouldn't the Whitewater falks stare in aghast?"[8])

In addition to Abigail's feared "ascilum" in Stockton, by 1870 there were two institutions for the insane in Oregon, and in Utah, on 19 February 1869, a territorial appropriation bill had authorized the amount of $5,000 "To be drawn by Salt Lake City to assist in erecting an Insane Asylum and Hospital." It was in the resulting asylum, sometime after 1

April 1876, that inmates worked a vibrant pieced quilt (no. 184).

The site selected for this new asylum was on the old Quarantine Grounds at the base of the Wasatch Mountains, just south of the entrance to Emigration Canyon, no longer the primary entry to the valley.[9] A day's distance from the city by oxen, the aspect of isolation (no. 185) would be consistent with the prevailing perception of the mentally ill as a source of potential danger, and a report to the city council would recommend "that strong cells be erected for the turbulent insane persons."[10] If that suggestion seems uncomfortably close to the conditions Abigail Malick described at the Stockton "ascilum," the description of the Utah hospital at its dedication seems far more humane. On 28 June 1870, President Brigham Young and other church elders of the Church of Jesus Christ of Latter-day Saints joined the city fathers to proceed by carriages approximately four miles from the city hall to the site of the asylum, traveling over "the road rather crooked, somewhat rough and very dusty, with a strong south wind prevailing" where they knelt in prayer and dedicated the ground.

The Asylum is a very neat, substantial, commodius, well finished and well arranged building, containing, I believe, 12 rooms, costing, with the hospital, in the neighborhood of $7,000.00. . . . There is a small farm surrounded by cedar posts, ready for the wire, which is on the ground to inclose it; two rows of shade trees encircle the front of the building, with a carriage drive between. From five to eight acres are under cultivation, crops looking well, but somewhat thinned by the late ravages of the "hoppers." A large number of fruit trees have been set out; but they are all badly damaged, and most of them ruined by the locusts. A large enclosure is being made where the unfortunates can have out-door exercise without the necessity of guarding. Everything seems well planned and thorough, with a view to comfort and weal of the occupants.[11]

Very little is known of what constituted "the weal of the occupants," for this was in all probability little more than a custodial facility. But we do know that quiltmaking was already an activity present in various public institutions across the country,[12] and six years later it was the type of enlightened therapy[13] brought to the Utah asylum by its new director, Dr. Seymour Bicknell Young (no. 185). Dr. Young, Brigham Young's nephew, had driven a team of oxen across the prairie to Utah in 1850 when he was thirteen years old; in 1874 he graduated third in a class of 208 from the College of Physicians and Surgeons of New York and returned to Salt Lake City to engage in private practice. The 17 March 1876 entry in his personal journal noted that "They are trying to add the title of Empress to Queen Victoria," that "The water was turned into the City water manes to day at 3PM," and that "Salt Lake City is trying to do away with its Insane Asylum by sending the patients all home to their respective counties." On 1 April 1876, "The Asylum & patients come under my charge from to day."[14]

The possibility that Dr. Young considered a variety of treatments for those patients is suggested by a newspaper clipping (no. 187) tucked into the pages of his journal, an advertisement for "Dr. E.C. West's Nerve and Brain Treatment, a guaranteed specific for [among other conditions] Softening of the Brain resulting in insanity and leading to misery, decay and death." But Dr. Young's son, Seymour B. Young Jr., remembered, "The inmates were taught to work where possible, for Dr. Young thought the mind

186. Undated photograph of Dr. Seymour Bicknell Young (1837–1924)
Courtesy Utah State Historical Society

should be kept busy to insure happiness. Many were taught craftsmanship. Others did those things adapted to them. The women — many of them — did needlework. One beautiful quilt is still in existence. The quilt has three thousand pieces and the designs are in many colors. There were some insane criminals of the most vicious type and they naturally had to be locked up most of the time. However the spirit of the asylum was that of consideration. . . . Many people, sent there, passed through the home of the afflicated and were made well."[15] This (see no. 184) is surely the quilt of which he spoke, the work of troubled minds soothed by the work of busy hands.

NOTES

1. Quoted in Lillian Schlissel's "The Malick Family in Oregon Territory," *Far from Home: Families of the Westward Journey* (New York: Schocken, 1989), 76.
2. Ibid., 75.
3. Ibid.
4. Ibid., 78.
5. Quoted in Kenneth L. Holmes, ed., *Covered Wagon Women: Diaries & Letters from the West-*

ern *Trails 1840–1890,* Vol. XI (Spokane, WA: Arthur H. Clark, 1993), p. 80.

6. Ibid., 25.

7. Ibid., 15.

8. Ibid., 51.

9. During the first ten years of settlement, Emigration Canyon was the main entrance into Salt Lake, but by 1860 entry was chiefly through Parley's Canyon to the South (called Parley's Golden Way, as it was briefly a toll road, the monies collected being used to support the maintenance of the road). The Quarantine Grounds held animals until it was found safe to let them mingle with the domestic herds and until legal ownership had been established. Conversation with Jay Hammond, Utah State Historical Society, 13 September 1994.

10. Quoted in Charles R. McKell, "The Utah State Hospital: A Study in the Care of the Mentally Ill," *Utah Historical Quarterly* 23 (1955): 300.

11. Jos. F. Smith. Letter to the Editor, *Deseret Evening News,* (29 June 1870): n.p.

12. In 1857, for example, an article in *Godey's Lady's Book* reported, "There is, in this State [Pennsylvania?], an institution for the reformation of girls who have been imprisoned for some crime; they are taught to sew neatly, and each one is allowed to exercise her taste and ingenuity in the manufacture of a patchwork quilt, which she is allowed to take away with her when she leaves. I have seen one hundred and fifty beds in this institution each covered with a different pattern of patchwork quilt; some were very tasteful and pretty, others not." Ellen Lindsay, "Patchwork," *Godey's Lady's Book* (February 1857): 166.

13. Women's magazines made frequent references to the unique mental benefits to be

187. Undated newspaper clipping
Courtesy Utah State Historical Society

derived from needlework. "Work is the best panacea for a mind diseased, tormented, or disturbed. To some temperments there is nothing so soothing and quieting as this lately revived, almost forgotten, art of our grandmothers—knitting. The quiet, even, regular motion of the needle quiets the nerves and tranquilizes the mind, and lets thoughts flow free." *Dorcas Magazine* (March 1884). In the middle of the next century, Dr. William Rush Dunton Jr. (self-described as a "physician to nervous ladies and an exponent of occupational therapy") collected clippings and photographs of quilts in order to interest his "nervous ladies" in quiltmaking. "It is easily understood that a nervous lady who is concentrating on making a quilt block has no time to worry over her fancied physical ill health or even over wrongs or slights which may be real, so that she is cultivating a more healthy mental attitude and habit." In addition to these references to his private patients, Dr. Dunton noted, "Even for those who must live in state hospitals because of their mental deterioration, sorting rags, cutting from patterns and other chores may bring contentment and aid in retarding deterioration." (William Rush Dunton Jr., M.D., *Old Quilts* (Catonsville, MD: published by the author, 1946), Introduction.

14. Seymour Bicknell Young's personal journal is in the collection of the Utah State Historical Society. Years of effort by the author and others to locate the records of the asylum have been ineffectual.

15. Seymour B. Young Jr., "The First State Mental Hospital," *Heartthrobs of the West,* compiled by Kate B. Carter, (Salt Lake City, UT: Daughters of Utah Pioneers, 1947), 340–41.

My Quilted Self

At the top of the quilt they worked together (no. 189), the Titus sisters embroidered "Pieced / by / Mary and Ruth Titus / Paternal / Aunts / For / Annie Davis / Titus / At birth / April 24, 1855." Lucky little Annie, to have such clever and loving aunts! But one may have been more clever than the other. Of the eighty smaller blocks that form its central field, approximately two dozen are quite standard motifs, several circled and some spoked, but none particularly distinctive; the remaining are figurative and floral, seemingly from the other's hands, intricate and imaginative, even in the rendering of the creatures of the field (no. 188); a cow's tail, for example, is decoratively braided, and the horse whose dappled body is the result of a carefully chosen cotton is fitted with embroidered bit, bridle, saddlebags, and stirrups.

America's artists had increasingly moved away from the formal portraits and landscapes of its European past, and four of the human figures that look out at us from this quilt are not unlike those other folk figures drawn and painted on paper and canvas during the middle of the nineteenth century.

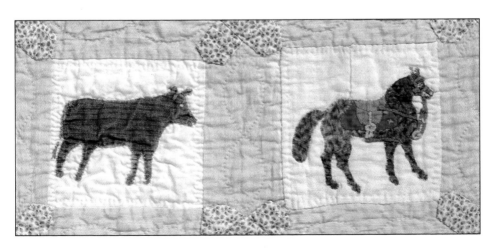

188. The Annie Titus Quilt (detail)

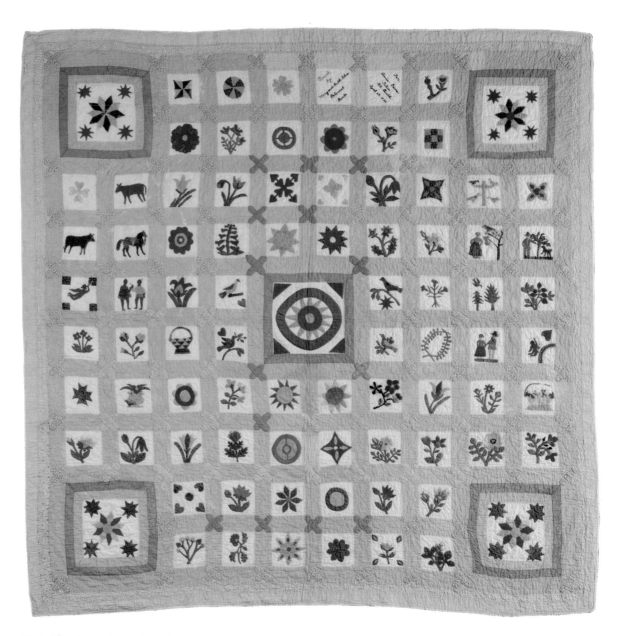

189. The Annie Titus Quilt
      "Pieced / by / Mary and Ruth Titus / Pater-
      nal / Aunts / For Annie Davis / Titus / At
      birth / April 24, 1855"
      United States
      Marked 1855
      73⅛ x 73⅛ in. (185.7 x 185.7 cm)
      Stella Rubin Antiques, Potomac, Maryland

190. The Annie Titus Quilt (detail)

tom of her bright red skirt.[1] Two children (no. 191) occupy themselves nearby. The boy plays with his curly tailed puppy and the girl, with her hands in her pockets, leans slightly toward a tree in which a bird feasts on the embroidered suggestion of small green leaves. (The bird's eye is a dot on the printed fabric from which its body is constructed, and the tree's very narrow trunk and limbs have been achieved through the use of reverse appliqué.)

In the following decade those young children, all joy and innocence, might have appeared in another family "album," a faded photograph (no. 192) evoking tender memories for those who loved them best. The textile on which these children stand is a lap robe, its woolen "star" motifs done in tufted yarn work.[2] By charming coincidence, a similar technique was also used on one of the blocks of Annie's quilt (no. 193) above another floral spray of delicate blossoms and buds and leaves.

One was perhaps the maker's quilted self, or a vision of little Annie as the young girl and woman she would grow to be. A man and woman are holding hands (no. 190), he with pocket and beard and top hat; she with tiny buttons down the front of her short green jacket and an embroidered band at the bot-

Children were sometimes photographed with objects related to their father's profession or occupation; perhaps the fruit that fills

(continued on p. 153)

191. The Annie Titus Quilt (detail)

192. Undated photograph
     Private Collection

193. The Annie Titus Quilt (detail)

194. The Ackerman Quilt (detail)

195. The Ackerman Quilt (detail)

196. The Ackerman Quilt
Vicinity of Saddle River, New Jersey
Marked 1859
96 x 72 in. (243.8 x 182.9 cm)
United Yarn Products

197. The Friendship Album Quilt
      Probably New Jersey or New York
      Marked 1879
      80 x 80 in. (203.2 x 203.2 cm)
      Courtesy of Sotheby's, Inc., New York City

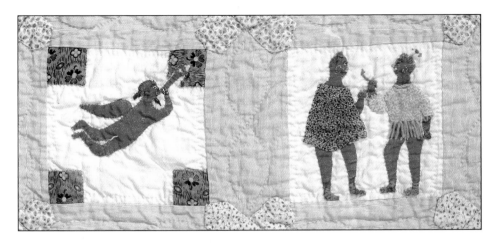

198. The Annie
Titus Quilt
(detail)

the basket placed in front of them and those they hold in their hands came from their father's orchards. Certainly that would have been the case had they been members of the Ackerman family near Saddle River, New Jersey. The fruit that appeared on two of the appliquéd blocks (nos. 194 and 195) of their quilt (no. 196) was certainly appropriate to the state in which it was made (New Jersey was then truly a garden state), and particularly appropriate to the family whose mem-

bers worked and/or signed the individual segments.[3] John Mowrefson was the oldest among them (we know he and his wife Maria were married in 1820), a prosperous farmer who would have sold the harvest of his fields and orchards (no. 194) to markets in Patterson, New Jersey, and in New York City. A block on another quilt thought to be worked within the extended Ackerman family holds a basket of strawberries and a basket of blackberries, and the quiltmaker, Betsy

199. The Friendship Album Quilt (detail)

200. The Friendship Album Quilt (detail)

201. The Friendship Album Quilt (detail)

202. The Child's Handkerchief Quilt (detail)
Late nineteenth century
92 x 90 in. (233.7 x 228.6 cm)
Laura Fisher/Antique Quilts & Americana,
NYC

Haring, has with great skill rendered each with attention to the particular shapes characteristic to that geographical area.[4]

Among those orchards in Saddle River were a number of horse farms, and the names of three brothers-in-law appear on blocks bearing images of that aspect of the regional scene. One (no. 195), its corners accentuated by bright, red apples, is signed "William Ackerman," the husband of the Mowrefsons' third daughter. Although the occasion that prompted the making of the quilt is unconfirmed, William's and Catharine's signatures are the only ones dated, "1859," possibly only coincidentally the year of their fifteenth wedding anniversary. It was through their family that the quilt descended.

New Jersey names and locations appear also on an appliquéd and embroidered friendship quilt (no. 197), joining others from Long Island, New York. In addition to the birds and blossoms that seem at times to be a compulsory component of this type of quilt,

an abundance of fanciful figures are contained within its scalloped border. Additional images on several of its blocks invite comparison to those on the Annie Titus quilt: the red angels (no. 198) on that quilt are red devils here (no. 199), but both quilts present stylized images of similarly garbed Native Americans (see no. 198) and (no. 200).

Just as the ladies of Philadelphia had found a particular printed peacock much to their liking (see "Presented by the Ladies"), an intriguing child's handkerchief seems also to have been a popular purchase, one from which the small figure of a young girl and her doll (no. 201) has been cut and applied to this album quilt. The handkerchief from which the image was cut (no. 202) was one of twenty-five of those small textiles that were set intact into a late-nineteenth-century quilt,[5] and it also inspired an appliquéd and embroidered block, "Dolly is Sick," on the Scenes of Childhood quilt (no. 203).[6]

NOTES

1. Human figures appearing on quilts in costume of the period was the subject of a major exhibition curated by the author at the Los Angeles County Museum of Art, October 18, 1990–January 13, 1991. For extensive illustration of such figures, see its accompanying publication, *Wrapped in Glory: Figurative Quilts & Bedcovers: 1700–1900* (New York: Thames and Hudson/Los Angeles County Museum of Art, 1990).

2. A Pennsylvania pillow top and examples of the type of tin templates used in the clipped-yarn construction of these motifs are illustrated in Nancy and Donald Roan, *Lest I Shall Be Forgotten* (Green Lane, PA: Goschenhoppen Historians, 1993), p. 70. Full quilts composed of woolen blocks with this motif are also found in Canada; one found in the Ottowa area is illustrated in Ruth McKendry, *Quilts and Other Bed Coverings in the Canadian Tradition* (Toronto: Van Nostrand Reinhold, 1979), 143. An Illinois example, circa 1900, is illustrated and discussed in E. Duane Elbert and Rachel Kamm Elbert, *History from the Heart: Quilt Paths Across Illinois* (Nashville: Rutledge Hill, 1993), 47.

3. Census and other records confirm that eleven of those who signed the twelve blocks (Catharine Ackerman, William A. Ackerman, Elisa Cooper, Catharine Depew, Aleta Jane Holstede, John J. Mowerson, John Mowrefson, Maria M. Mowrefson, William Pulis, Laweesa Winter, Peter H. Winter) were bound together by birth or marriage. Most were members of the Saddle River Reformed Church, and three of the couples were married there. *New Jersey Census Records* (1850); *The Kakiat Patent in Bergen County, New Jersey*, published privately by Howard I. Durie; the *D.A.D. Newsletter, David Ackerman Descendants–1662;* and personal communication with Katharine P. Randall, Bergen County Historical Society, River Edge, New Jersey, 17 June 1989.

4. This quilt is in the collection of the Bergen County Historical Society and I am indebted

203. The Scenes of Childhood Quilt (detail)
Fourth quarter nineteenth century
37 x 35 in. (94 x 88.9 cm)
Private Collection
Photo courtesy of America Hurrah Antiques, NYC

to Kevin Wright, curator of Steuben House, River Edge, New Jersey, for having provided these descriptive details. It is illustrated in *The Tree of Life: Selections from Bergen County Folk Art*, published by the society in 1983.

5. Illustrated in full in Judith Reiter Weissman and Wendy Lavitt, *Labors of Love: America's Textiles and Needlework, 1650–1930* (New York: Knopf, 1987), 200.

6. For a full illustration of the "Scenes of Childhood Quilt" and its related pillowcase, see Sandi Fox, *Small Endearments: Nineteenth-Century Quilts for Children and Dolls* (Nashville: Rutledge Hill, 1994), 152–55. Additional children's handkerchiefs are illustrated and discussed throughout.

204. Sister Hattie Nye's Quilt
Made by members of the relief society for
presentation to Harriet (Hattie) Maria Hor-
spool Nye
San Francisco, California
Blocks dated 1899, presented February 1900
68 x 61 in. (172.7 x 154.9 cm)
Museum of Church History and Art, Salt
Lake City

To Labor in God's Vineyard

The journals in which those very early quiltmakers had recorded the beginnings of their craft[1] were of diverse material and design, and their usually careful construction was what they, and their peers, and indeed we might expect of their quilts. In Hadley, Massachusetts, Elizabeth Phelps's diary (begun in Boston in 1763) spanned fifty-four years, filling a number of pamphlets, each made by hand, the numbered pages sewn together and bound in coarse paper covers bearing the date of beginning and concluding entries;[2] Francis Baylor Hill's Virginia journal covered only one brief year at Hillsborough, and is a "small book of folded leaves of light-weight laid paper, sewn into the gatherings, approximately 6½" across the page by 7¾" down."[3] And as the nineteenth century turned into the next there was bound into a handmade pamphlet[4] of stained blue paper tied with now-soiled gold ribbon an extraordinary document filled with the kind of detailed primary information we are generally denied regarding those earlier efforts. It is a letter dated 9 February 1900, written in San Francisco, to Sister Hattie Nye:[5]

About three years ago there came to this City to labor in God's Vineyard, President Nye and Sister Nye, and I cannot

help but say as I look back o'er the past, that, as the rose, "on the tree of acquaintance, the bud of friendship has blossomed into love."

And, as Sister Nye has labored with us Sisters in the Relief Society during this time most faithfully, there came to my mind an idea of in some small way of showing our love, and as I dwelt on the thought, it did seem to me that if each dear sister of the Mission would assist, that something might be made in which all could have a part, and which might be joined in one large whole. Then it was that I did think of a Souvenir Quilt. Each sister could make a block and they could be put together in one large spread, and I wish to state here, before proceeding further, that we are much indebted to dear Sister Hughes for her kind assistance in purchasing materials with which to make the Quilt complete. She was one of the first to enthuse and has shown her love in a most substantial way.

I have gathered the blocks in and arranged them, as you will soon see, in a most handsome quilt (no. 204); and I

205. Sister Hattie Nye's Quilt (detail)

am sure, dear Sister Nye, that with each stitch that has been placed in the blocks, has been done with a loving thought of you, and for myself I would say that as I did gather them in and join them in one large whole, with each stitch I have thought most tenderly and lovingly of you and how you have been our bright sunbeam these past few years, and have asked God to bless you and dear Brother Nye in your work, so that truly you can call it a loving "souvenir" of your sojourn in the Golden State of California amongst us, and which may last long after we are laid to our eternal rest,
> "And the cares that infest the day,
> Shall fold their tents like the Arab
> And silently steal away."

And which may also pass down to your children and, possibly, childrens children, that they might know of the love borne their Mother while she labored in our midst.

Here, within this quilt, dear sister, you will find blocks (no. 205) with loving thoughts from sisters in the Northern part of the State, some from the Southern part of the state, some from our own city, San Francisco, and adjoining cities, and even from sisters in dear Utah; so they have come from far and near and speak of love from each one therein represented.

I feel that God has blessed your mission to the State and that both of you have been a blessing to all with whom you have come in contact. You have ever heeded the call of the sick and afflicted, comforted those in sore distress, and endeavored to teach the correct and right way to walk with God and become children of his kingdom; showing that it is not all of life to live, nor all of death to die; that there is a life hereafter where all the Saints shall meet again, and I pray God to grant his richest blessings unto you and yours and may you yet labor in this field, which so needs you, for a long time to come.

The last stitches have been placed within this quilt as I have sat up in my bed of illness and at the present writing it is very doubtful if I will be able to be with you at the presentation; the spirit is willing but the flesh is weak, and yet I will be there in thought and when this is read by my Grandson, you will feel that I am there, and in closing I would say unto the brothers and sisters here gathered, this
> "Count the day lost, whose low
> descending sun
> Views at thy hands, no worthy
> action done."

[signed] Sister Isabel Y. Sewell

206. Sister Hattie Nye's Quilt (detail)

In her letter, Isabel Sewell told Hattie, and us, of a silk and velvet quilt worked for purpose and for pleasure; on the quilt block she herself constructed and signed, a young woman painted on silk waves to us across the century (no. 206).

NOTES

1. See pp. 3–7.
2. Elizabeth Porter Phelps. "The Diary of Elizabeth (Porter) Phelps." Edited by Thomas Eliot Andrews. *The New England Historical and Genealogical Register* (January 1964), 5.
3. Frances Baylor Hill, "The Diary of Frances Baylor Hill of 'Hillsborough,' King and Queen County, Virginia" (1797). From the introduction to the transcription edited by William K. Bottorff and Roy C. Flannagan in *Early American Literature Newsletter* 2, No. 3 (Winter 1967), 5.
4. In the research files of the Museum of Church History and Art, Salt Lake City.

5. Hattie Nye's family was among the great number of Mormon converts to emigrate from England to Utah in the mid-1850s, and she was one of those pioneer children who "walked and walked and walked." She married Ephraim Hesmer Nye, an employee of the Central Pacific Railroad, on 9 February 1867, just after her twentieth birthday. "Eph" was called by the Church of Jesus Christ of Latter-day Saints to serve as president of the California mission, and Hattie joined him distinguished by the fact that she had been issued the first certificate given to a sister missionary of the church. In San Francisco, she served as the relief society president of the mission (called the ladies aid society at that time). Their period of service completed, Hattie and "Eph" returned to Salt Lake City, ready to bear testimony as to the success of their California experience. Hattie carried this quilt with her as tangible proof of the way in which she had touched the lives of those with whom she had "labored in God's Vineyard." Object file, Museum of Church History and Art.

Bibliography

Allen, Gloria Seaman. *First Flowerings: Early Virginia Quilts.* Exhibition Catalogue. Washington, DC: DAR Museum, 1987.

American Folk Paintings: Paintings and Drawings Other Than Portraits from the Abby Aldrich Rockefeller Folk Art Center. The Abby Aldrich Rockefeller Folk Art Center Series, edited by Beatrice T. Rumford, no. 2. Boston: Little, Brown, in association with the Colonial Williamsburg Foundation, 1988.

Ammons, Betty. Letter to Mrs. Thomas H. Morgan, 29 July 1994.

An Account of the Commemoration of the Twenty-Fifth Anniversary of the Boston Street M. E. Church, Lynn, Mass., May 20, 1878. Lynn, MA: n.p., 1880.

Annals of Pioneer Settlers on the Whitewater and its Tributaries in the Vicinity of Richmond, Ind., from 1804 to 1830. Richmond, IN: Press of the Telegram Printing Company, 1875.

Applegate, Jesse. *Recollections of My Boyhood.* Roseburg, OR: Press of Review Publishing, 1914.

Arthur, T. S. "The Quilting Party," in *Godey's Lady's Book,* September 1849.

Atkins, Jacqueline Marx. *Shared Threads: Quilting Together–Past and Present.* New York: Viking Studio Books, 1994.

Ayer, Sarah Connell. *The Diary of Sarah Connell Ayer.* Portland, ME: Lefavor-Tower, 1910.

Baltimore *American,* December 17–22, 1846.

Baumgarten, Linda. *Eighteenth-Century Clothing at Williamsburg.* Williamsburg, VA: Colonial Williamsburg, 1986.

Blum, Dilys, and Jack L. Lindsey. "Nineteenth-Century Appliqué Quilts." *Philadelphia Museum of Art Bulletin* 85, nos. 363/364 (Fall 1989).

Boardman, Nancy. "The Diaries of Nancy Ellen Boardman." *Historical Collections of the Danvers Historical Society* 29 (1941): 54–74.

Burns, Sarah. *Pastoral Inventions: Rural Life in Nineteenth-Century American Art and Culture.* Philadelphia: Temple University Press, 1989.

Charles City County, VA. Record, 1766–1774 (22 April 1773), 459.

Cleveland, Richard L., and Donna Bister. *Plain and Fancy: Vermont's People and Their Quilts as a Reflection of America.* Gualala, CA: Quilt Digest Press, 1991.

Cozart, Dorothy. "A Century of Fundraising Quilts: 1860–1960," *Uncoverings* 5 (1984).

D.A.D. Newsletter, David Ackerman Descendants–1662.

Davenport, Sarah. "The Journal of Sarah Davenport: May 1, 1849 Through May 16, 1852." *New Canaan Historical Society Annual* 2 (1950): 26–89.

Deseret Evening News, 9 February 1900.

Dorcas Magazine, December 1884.

Dorcas Magazine, March 1884.

Dunton, William Rush Jr., *Old Quilts.* Catonsville, MD. Published by the author, 1946.

Durie, Howard I. *The Kakiat Patent in Bergen County, New Jersey.* Published for the author, n.d.

Elbert, E. Duane, and Rachel Kamm Elbert. *History from the Heart: Quilt Paths Across Illinois.* Nashville: Rutledge Hill, 1993.

Fogg, Alonzo J. *The Statistics and Gazetteer of New-Hampshire.* Concord, NH: D. L. Guernsey, 1874.

Fox, Sandi. *Nineteenth-Century Quilts for Children and Dolls.* Second Edition. Nashville: Rutledge Hill, 1994.

———. *Wrapped in Glory: Figurative Quilts & Bedcovers 1700–1900.* New York: Thames and Hudson/Los Angeles County Museum of Art, 1990.

Garvan, Beatrice B., and Charles F. Hummel. *The Pennsylvania Germans: A Celebration of Their Arts 1683–1850.* Exhibition Catalogue. Philadelphia: Philadelphia Museum of Art, 1982.

Gibbens, Byrd. "Charles and Maggie Brown in Colorado and New Mexico, 1880–1930," in *Far from Home: Families of the Westward Journey.* New York: Schocken, 1989.

Goldsborough, Jennifer F. "Baltimore Album Quilts," *The Magazine Antiques,* March 1994.

Goodrich, Frank B. *The Tribute Book: A Record of The Munificence, Self-Sacrifice and Patriotism of the American People During the War for the Union.* New York: Derby & Miller, 1865.

Hanks, David, and Page Talbott. "Daniel Pabst: Philadelphia Cabinet Maker." *Philadelphia Museum of Art Bulletin* 73, no. 316 (April 1977).

Hartley, Florence. *The Ladies' Hand Book of Fancy and Ornamental Work.* Philadelphia: J. W. Bradley, 1861.

Hewett, David. "Unusual Use of Marking Devices Produces Rarities," *Maine Antique Digest,* September 1993.

Hill, Frances Baylor. "The Diary of Frances Baylor Hill of 'Hillsborough,' King and Queen County, Virginia (1797)." Edited by William K. Bottorff and Roy C. Flannagan. *Early American Literature Newsletter* 2, no. 3 (Winter 1967).

Holmes, Kenneth L., ed. *Covered Wagon Women: Diaries & Letters from the Western Trails.* 11 Volumes (Glendale, CA, and Spokane, WA: Arthur H. Clark, 1983–93.)

Hurst, Ronald L. Letter to the author, 5 October 1994.

Indiana Quilt Registry Project. *Quilts of Indiana: Crossroads of Memories.* Bloomington: Indiana University Press, 1991.

J. W. B. *Metropolitan Life Unveiled: Sunlight and Shadow of America's Great Cities.* Philadelphia: West Philadelphia, 1891.

Katzenberg, Dena S. *Baltimore Album Quilts.* Exhibition Catalogue. Baltimore: Baltimore Museum of Art, 1981.

Kellogg, Fanny. *Typhrena Ely White's Journal, Being a Record, Written One Hundred Years Ago, of the Daily Life of a Young Lady of Puritan Heritage.* New York: Grafton, 1904.

Kolter, Jane Bentley. *Forget Me Not: A Gallery of Friendship and Album Quilts.* New York: Sterling, 1990.

Larcom, Lucy. *A New England Girlhood: Outlined from Memory.* Boston: Houghton, Mifflin, 1892.

Laury, Jean Ray. *Ho For California! Pioneer Women and Their Quilts.* New York: Dutton, 1990.

Lewis, Alonzo, and James R. Newhall. *History of Lynn, Essex County, Massachusetts.* Boston: John L. Shorey, 1865.

Lindsay, Ellen. "Patchwork," *Godey's Lady's Book and Magazine,* February 1857.

Mason, Lizzie Norton, and James Duncan Phillips, eds. "The Journal of Elizabeth Cranch," *Essex Institute Historical Collections* 80, no. 1 (1944): 1–36.

McKell, Charles R. "The Utah State Hospital: A Study in the Care of the Mentally Ill," *Utah Historical Quarterly* 23, 1955.

McKendry, Ruth. *Quilts and Other Bed Coverings in the Canadian Tradition.* Toronto: Van Nostrand Reinhold, 1979.

Meredith, William Henry, ed., *An Account of the Fifty-First Anniversary of the Boston Street Methodist Episcopal Church, and of Methodist Beginnings in Lynn, Massachusetts.* Published for the church, 1904.

Middlesex County, VA. Will Book C, 1740–1748 (30 July 1747), 379.

"Minutes of the Female Missionary Society of the First Baptist Church of Philadelphia." n.p., n.d.

Montgomery, Florence M. *Printed Textiles: English and American Cottons and Linens 1700–1850.* New York: Viking, 1970.

Moss, Gillian. *Printed Textiles 1760–1860 in the Collection of the Cooper-Hewitt Museum.* Exhibition Catalogue. Washington, DC: Smithsonian Institution, 1987.

Mrs. F. A. W. "Autograph Quilts," *Good Housekeeping,* 26 October 1889.

National Gallery of Art. *An American Sampler: Folk Art from the Shelburne Museum.* Exhibition Catalogue. Washington, DC: National Gallery of Art, 1987.

Nicoll, Jessica F. *Quilted for Friends: Delaware Valley Signature Quilts, 1840–1855.* Exhibition Catalogue. Winterthur, DE: Winterthur Museum, 1986.

Old Print Showcase, Vol. 7, no. 1, (January–February 1980).

100th Anniversary Booklet of the First Congregational Church, Canandaigua, N.Y. n.p., June 1899.

Ordonez, Margaret T. "Ink Damage on Nineteenth-Century Cotton Signature Quilts," *Uncoverings* 13 (1992)

Phelps, Elizabeth Porter. "The Diary of Elizabeth Porter Phelps." Edited by Thomas Eliot Andrews. *The New England Historical and Genealogical Register* 118 (1964): 3–30, 108–27, 217–36, 297–308; 119 (1965): 43–59, 127–40, 205–23, 289–307; 120 (1966): 57–63, 128–35, 203–14, 293–304; 121 (1967): 57–69, 95–100, 296–303; 122 (1968): 62–70, 115–23, 220–27, 302–09.

Pramberg, Noreen C. Letter to the author, 30 March 1992.

Propps, J. J. "My Childhood and Youth in Arkansas," *Arkansas Historical Quarterly* 2, no. 4 (Winter 1967).

Randall, Katharine P. Letter to the author, 17 June 1989.

Richards, Caroline Cowles. *Village Life in America 1852–1872: including the Period of the American Civil War as told in the Diary of a School-Girl.* Williamsburg, MA: Corner House, 1972.

Ring, Betty. *American Needlework Treasures.* New York: Dutton, 1987.

Roan, Nancy, and Donald Roan. *Lest I Shall Be Forgotten.* Green Lane, PA: Goschenhoppen Historians, 1993.

Ross, Nancy Wilson. *Westward the Women.* San Francisco: North Point, 1985.

Sanborn, Melinda Lutz. *Lost Babes: Fornication Abstracts from Court Records, Essex County, Massachusetts 1692–1745.* Derry, NH: n.p., 1992.

Scharf, J. Thomas. *History of Baltimore City and County.* Philadelphia: Louis H. Everts, 1881.

Schlissel, Lillian. "The Malick Family in Oregon Territory" in *Far from Home: Families of the Westward Journey.* New York: Schocken, 1989.

Scourse, Nicolette. *The Victorians and their Flowers.* London: Croom Helm, 1989.

Smith, Jos. F. Letter to the Editor, *Deseret Evening News,* 29 June 1870.

Smith-Rosenberg, Carroll. "The Female World of Love and Ritual: Relations between Women in Nineteenth-Century America," *Signs: Journal of Women in Culture and Society* 1, no. 1 (1975).

Spencer, H. C. *Spencerian Key to Practical Penmanship.* New York: Ivison, Blakeman, Taylor, 1879.

Tree of Life: Selections from Bergen County Folk Art. Bergen County (NJ) Historical Society, 1983.

Trollope, Frances. *Domestic Manners of the Americans.* London: Whittaker, Treacher, 1832.

Ulrich, Laurel Thatcher. *A Midwife's Tale: The Life of Martha Ballard, Based on Her Diary 1785–1812.* New York: Vintage, 1991.

Vital Records of Newbury Massachusetts to the End of the Year 1849, Vol. II, Part 1. Salem, MA: Essex Institute, 1911.

Weissman, Judith Reiter, and Wendy Lavitt. *Labors of Love: America's Textiles and Needlework, 1650–1930.* New York: Knopf, 1987.

White, William Allen. "The 'Quilting Bee' Crowd," in *History of Butler County, Kansas.* Edited by Vol. P. Mooney. Lawrence, KS: Standard, 1916.

Whitford, Maria Langworthy. *— And A White Vest for Sam'l: An Account of Rural Life in Western N.Y. from the diaries of Maria Langworthy Whitford of Alfred Station, N.Y. 1857–1861.* Edited by Helene C. Phelan. Alfred, NY: Sun, 1976.

Whittock, Nathaniel. *The Art of Drawing and Colouring from Nature, Flowers, Fruit, and Shells; To Which Is Added, Correct Directions for Preparing the Most Brilliant Colours for Painting on Velvet, with the Mode of Using Them; Also, the New Method of Oriental Tinting.* London: Isaac Taylor Hinton, 1829.

Williams, Hermann Warner Jr. *Mirror to the American Past: A Survey of American Genre Painting: 1750–1900.* Greenwich, CT: New York Graphic Society, 1973.

Winslow, Anna Green. *Diary of Anna Green Winslow: A Boston School Girl of 1771.* Edited by Alice Morse Earle. Boston: Houghton, Mifflin, 1894.

Young, Seymour Bicknell. Journal. Utah State Historical Society, Salt Lake City.

Young, Seymour B. Jr., "The First State Mental Hospital." In *Heartthrobs of the West.* Compiled by Kate B. Carter. Salt Lake City: Daughters of Utah Pioneers, 1947.

Zegart, Shelly. "Old Maid, New Woman," *The Quilt Digest* 4 (1986).

Index

aid societies, 97, 99, 100, 103–04, 109, 111
"a quilting," 3
A Quilting Bee in the Olden Time, 104
albums, 15, 22, 39, 68, 149
album quilts, 9, 29, 35, 53, 59, 78, 135, 140–41, 154
America, colonial, 9
Annals of Pioneer Settlers on the Whitewater and its Tributaries, 81
appliqué, 27, 31, 39, 44, 48, 53, 57, 59, 63, 64, 66, 67, 81, 89, 93, 107, 115, 130, 149, 153, 154
apple parings, 8
A Quilting Party in Western Virginia, 8
asylums, 143–46
autograph albums, 83

Baltimore, MD, 51–62
Baptist, 39, 41
bedcover, 115
bedquilts, 3–4, 5, 6, 78, 103
biblical, 39, 66, 74, 77, 83, 109, 111, 115
Boston Street Aid Society, 97–101, 104
Boston Style of Writing, 29
botany, 39
Breaking Home Ties, 75
broderie perse, 6, 16, 36, 51, 55

calico, 66
Carolina Lilys, 93
cartouche, 71
chintz, 39, 41, 42, 44, 47, 109
church, 107
Church of Jesus Christ of Latter-day Saints, 103, 144, 145
Civil War, 100
clothing, 3, 22, 25, 120, 123, 135
Colonial Williamsburg Foundation, 15
Connecticut, 7
cottons, 44, 63, 88, 89, 107
"counterpain," 6–7

dedicatory blocks, 84
Delaware, 63
Delaware Valley, 48
Delectable Mountains, 83, 88
diaries (journals), 3, 4–5, 7, 27, 77–78, 127, 143–44, 157–59
Domestic Manners of the Americans, 78
Dorcas Magazine, 21
Douglass, Frederick, 113
Dunton, William Rush, Jr., 57

embellishment, 22, 25, 88, 93, 128

fabrics, dress, 22
fashion, 53
finishing, 25
First Congregational Church, 78, 80
fondu, 54
frakturs, 115
friendship quilts, 9, 35, 89, 91, 93, 154
fundraising, 41–42, 107, 109–13

Garfield, James A., 89, 91
German migration, 63
Gleason's Pictorial Drawing-Room Companion, 8
Godey's Lady's Book and Magazine, 8, 22, 123
Good Housekeeping, 107

Harper's Weekly, 8
Hurst, Ronald L., 15
husking bees, 8
huswif, 16

Illinois, 133, 135
Indiana, 109, 113
ink, 27, 29, 30–31, 71, 97, 116
insanity, 143–46
Iowa, 143

journals. *See* diaries

Kansas, 9–11
Krimmel, John, 7, 8, 9

ladies societies, 98, 109, 111
La Mode illustrée, 72
Larcom, Lucy, 42, 129
"Laurel Leaves," 31

mail-order patterns, 86
marriage, 78
Marseilles quilting, 6
Maryland, Baltimore, 53, 55, 56, 57
Massachusetts, 3, 4, 21, 27, 64, 111, 129, 157
memories of quilting, 10
Methodist, 56, 97, 101, 103, 107, 109, 111
Mexican War, 56
migration, 133, 134, 136, 139–40
Miller, Lewis, 15
Missouri, 133
monograms, 71
mortality, 119–26
motherhood, 74
motifs, 147–55: acorns, 63, 71, 111; birds, 47, 59, 66,
    67–68; botanical, 53; flags, 89, 91; floral, 16, 21–22,
    35, 36, 39, 41, 42, 44, 47, 48, 51, 53, 54, 57, 59, 64, 71,
    93, 103, 115, 116, 120, 124, 147, 149; funerary, 56;
    leaves, 31, 42, 63, 64, 71, 109, 116; Masonic, 57; pea-
    cocks, 42; shells, 44; stars, 116, 149; wreaths, 36, 39,
    41, 44
Mount, William Sidney, 8
mourning, 42, 47, 48, 89, 115–17, 120, 124, 132, 133

New Jersey, 36, 42, 84, 88, 139
New York, 15, 35, 78, 135

Oak Leaf and Reel, 63
Oak leaves, 63, 71, 111
Ohio, 35, 57, 89, 91
old maids, 77, 81
ombre, 54
Orbis Pictus, 15
Oregon Territory, 113, 143
Overland trail, 115, 133

patterns, 71–72, 73
Payson's Indelible Ink, 27, 29
penmanship, 29
Pennsylvania, 15, 35, 36, 47, 63, 91, 133
penny blocks, 109
Perry, Enoch Wood, 8, 9
petticoats, quilted, 3, 4
preachers, 35

Presbyterian, 35

Quaker, 3, 42, 44, 47, 57, 63, 88
Queen Victoria, 39
"quilt," 3
quilting bees, 8
quilting circles, 127–28
quilting frame, 4, 128
Quilting Frolic, 7, 9
quilting parties, 8

Rhode Island, 119
Ringgold, Maj. Samuel, 55–56
rose, moss, 36–37, 39

sampler quilt, 93
Sawteeth, 93
Sewing Society Quilt, 41
seashells, 41–2
signatures (signing), 27, 29–31, 47, 64, 88, 93, 107, 111,
    147, 154, 159
signing. *See* signatures
silk, 47, 54, 88, 115, 119
Single sisterhood, 77, 123
social causes, 107
Spencer, Platte, R., 29
Spencerian System of Practical Penmanship, 29
spinster, 80–81
Spiritualism, 127–32
stencils, 29–31
Stone, Lucy, 113

temperance, 111, 113
textiles, 54, 120, 123
The Quilting Party, 8
The Schoolmistress, 81
toiles, pictorial, 13
Trollope, Frances, 78

United Methodist Historical Society, 27
United States Sanitary Commission, 100–01

Victorian, 51, 78, 83, 124
Virginia, 4, 25, 83, 131, 157

Watson, Lt.-Col. William H., 52–57
wheel-type patterns, 107
Whittock, Nathaniel, 36
whole-cloth, 3
Wisconsin, 139
Woman's Christian Temperance Union, 113
wool, 54

Young Ladies Sewing Society, 78